ARE YOU BORG NOW?

SAID SHAIYE

Book design by Kevin Barrett Kane

Author Photo: Ali Salah

International Standard Book Number: 978-0-578-91546-3

Are You Borg Now? ———

Bismillahi Rahmaani Raheem.

In the name of Allah, the Most Beneficent, the Most Merciful.

I begin this book as a Muslim, by bearing witness that there is no God but Allah, and that Muhammad (Peace Be Upon Him) is his Prophet and Messenger. I ask that Allah bless our Beloved Prophet, his family, his offspring, his descendants, his companions, and his ummah.

I give thanks to my Lord for blessing me with the gift of writing, which has helped me weather many a dark storm. I give thanks to my family who has helped me through more rough patches than I can count.

I give thanks to my friends and supporters, both literary and otherwise. I give thanks, because without gratitude there can be no progress.

Any benefit that comes from this book is due to Allah and Allah alone. Any shortcomings that come from this book are due to my own human weakness.

There are themes of hopelessness and other not very Islamic things discussed in this book. Before you judge me, know that I am committed first and foremost to my humanity. I believe in transparency and recognize that the sum of my life experiences have led me to be the man I am today.

I believe that I am greater for having survived various periods of turmoil in which my faith was tested. I believe that had I not gone through them, I would not have the strength to preserve the pain of my life, the pain of being Muslim in this world today.

I know many a Muslim who is struggling to reconcile their faith with the trappings of modernity, and an ingrained inferiority complex brought upon by decades and centuries of anti-Muslim propaganda. It's hard out here for a believer. We down bad.

I hope that these pages, should they find you, serve as a reminder that Allah is in control, and that no matter how dark the road gets, the light will surely return. This is the promise of Allah, and the promise of our Faith.

Islam is what holds me together and I don't believe in pretending to be anything I'm not.

I am a survivor of childhood trauma, of genocide, of civil war. I am a survivor of serious addiction who still to this day struggles with his mental health. I am a believer and I give thanks for all of this. It makes me the person I am, and it has led me to be a thoughtful and caring person.

I care for other's pain because the central theme of my life has been pain. I hold my people in ways they are incapable of holding me. I care for my Muslim brothers and sisters struggling to hold onto their faith in these hot coal times.

Too many of our institutions have turned their back on us – the young, the struggling, the hopeless. We have heard that it's just a matter of willpower, and that we just need to be better Muslims & our problems will go away. My question is: what is a Muslim who does not struggle? I find that the struggle, in and of itself, is that which, if not defines, refines our faith.

People who've never had a serious addiction sometimes can't understand that addiction is not a choice. That praying extra prayers won't automatically make that addiction disappear. Faith is critical to recovery, because faith gives us hope, and hope keeps us from going back. And Allah's blessings are critical to recovery, for nothing happens without His consent.

But we cannot replace the hard work needed to recover & find one's way back to sobriety – the skill building needed, the changing of environments & cutting off of friends – with a simple "just pray and you'll be fine" mantra.

Yes, absolutely pray. But what do you do when you pray and you're still not fine? What then? Well, that's when you write, or read, or go to therapy, or rehab, or whatever it takes for you to find some peace. You never let go of your prayers, no matter what. You never stop confiding in Allah. You never stop believing He will help you, because He will – and that is His promise, and Allah's promise is always fulfilled.

So, I guess what I'm trying to say is: it's hard to understand what it means to be a young Muslim person in the West. People expect us to be perfect, while we're struggling with more temptations and doubts than our (often immigrant) parents likely did. People don't understand how hard it is for us, how much deprogramming we have to do to maintain our faith.

People don't get that there's an all-out war for the hearts and minds of Muslim children – that there are all types of movements and isms that are trying to rob our kids of their faith. People think that just going through the motions of what worked for our parents "back home" is enough to save us in our new reality. And the reality is, most of us have no concept of home outside of the west.

We are the displaced children of displaced children, and we suffer from an additional displacement in our hearts, preventing us from fully connecting with our Faith unless we do serious work therein.

I've felt so hopeless and lost in my life. And I recognize that Allah was with me every step of the way, even when I thought myself to be forsaken and abandoned. Allah would never abandon one of His servants.

I pray that you find the answers you seek, no matter where they come from. And I pray that the pain in your heart eases. Keep your heart to Allah, and keep your pen to page. Keep letting it out. Keep letting that ink flow, dropping like tears staining your writing pad. And pray.

U.S. Department of Justice

Immigration and Naturalization Service

AMERICAN EMBASSY NAIROBI
BOX 21
APO NY 09675

AMERICAN EMBASSY
P. O. BOX 30137
NAIROBI, KENYA

NAME: Sofia Hassan Jama

DATE: 1 0 JUL 1995

ADDRESS: _____

Dear Applicant:

The U.S. Immigration and Naturalization Service (INS) has determined that you are eligible for resettlement in the United States as a refugee under Section 207 of the U.S. Immigration and Nationality Act.

Now that INS has approved your eligibility, you will need a medical examination. Chest x-rays will also be required. Please contact the International Organization for Migration. They are located on Amboseli Road (off Gitanga Road) Nairobi, for your medical appointment. Office hours are from 8 A.M - 12 P.M Monday through Friday. The examination will be free of charge. The results of the medical examination will be sent directly to this office.

Arrangements will be made for you to have four photographs taken, which should be given to the medical doctor. The doctor will not examine you without the photographs.

When all admission requirements are completed, and this office has received authority to do so, travel to the United States will be arranged for you. Your name will then appear on a travel list posted at the J.V.A office.

You should then report to I.O.M for final exit clearances on the date indicated on the travel list. You must also report for Cultural Orientation Classes on the scheduled dates. These dates are posted at J.V.A and I.O.M.

"Report to I. O. M. on 1 1 JUL 1995

Sincerely,

Officer in Charge

Mohamed Farah Shaiye
Said Mohamed Farah
Liban Mohamed Farah
Abdirazak Mohamed Farah

01/95
NRB

5/221

| 1. | Name: | (First) *SAID* | (Middle) *MOHAMED* | (Last) *FARAH* |

1.	Name:	(First) SAID	(Middle) MOHAMED (Last) FARAH

2.	Present address:	SUMMER VIEW. EASTLEIGH. TEL - 760479 NBI.

3.	Date of birth: (month/day/year)	Place of birth (city or town)	(Province)	(Country)	Present nationality:
	5/22/	MOGADISHU	BENADIR	SOMALIA	SOMALIA.

4.	Country from which I fled or was displaced : SOMALIA	On or about (month/day/year): APR. 1991.

5. Reasons (State in detail):

I WAS VERY LITTLE (2.5 YRS OF AGE ONLY) AND CAN'T REMEMBER MUCH ABOUT THE WAR.

Naomi Wildman.

Explain?

She was this little girl that was born on Voyager, exactly how was never made clear. But she has anxiety about going back to Earth.

In what way?

Voyager, as you already know, has been wandering the Delta Quadrant for a couple of years now, trying to get back to the Alpha, on the other side of the Milky Way. It's gonna take almost 70 years at maximum warp. And this little girl, Naomi Wildman, her entire world is the inside of this ship.

She's never seen Earth?

Wouldn't know what to do with it if she did. In her spare time, she hangs out in the Astrometrics Lab with Seven of Nine, asking her annoying questions. It's always fun to watch them interact. Seven, this person who's rediscovering what it means to be human and talks like a robot in clipped, terse sentences – recreation is irrelevant, fun is inefficient – and Naomi, this curious little seven-year-old asking annoying questions. Deep Sigh.

What's wrong?

I'm sick to my stomach again.

What's on your mind?

I'm not sure, but it's some type of anxiety. Also, I really don't want to write today.

Then walk away, I won't be mad at you.

I knew you'd understand.

If not me, who else?

Allah.

Allah will always be there for us. Know that.

Fa sho that.

$$* \quad * \quad *$$

Naomi Wildman.

Explain?

Why are Seven and her mannerisms so interesting to you?

Something about her speaks to me.

The way she talked, maybe.

Yeah, and also her emotional sterility. It's like she… could feel emotions, but her emotional lexicon was limited. Think of her as an adult with a child's understanding of emotions.

Sure sounds like someone I know.

Yeah, I know. It's me.

What did your last therapist say?

That I have a limited emotional vocabulary.

Said of Nine.

I like that. Catch me in my regeneration alcove, getting sleep.

How'd you sleep last night, bruh?

Terrible. Heater was too high, I had on too many layers, didn't drink enough water yesterday.

Woke up dehydrated and icky, didn't ya?

Affirmative. And Wingstop. A 6-piece lemon-pepper boneless combo with fries and a Barq's root beer right before bed made my stomach do flips in my dreams.

You and that stomach.

I eat emotionally.

You've said that before.

I feel like I'm getting bored of this format.

It's not really going anywhere. We're kind of stuck. I think you're afraid of trying new things.

Even when I'm trying new things?

It's not swimming if you're using floaties.

I can attest to the fact that Mohamed Shaiye and Safia Jama are the parents of Said, Liban and Abdirizak Farah because Safia Jama is my sister. I knew Mohamed Shaiye before he married my sister. I was present at their wedding in 1986 in Mogadishu Somalia. It was a special wedding for Moslem people. At the wedding we cooked, slaughtered goats. Both our families came together for the wedding. The wedding was at our family's home in Mogadishu. The wedding lasts about five or six hours after that the new married couple are taken their new home.

My sister came to America in 1995 and I came to America in 1999. I first came to Georgia where my mother and some of my brothers and sisters. Later I came to Seattle. When I came to Seattle I met up with my sister and her family here. I live in Seatac and my sister lives in Seattle.

Why do you write?

I'm afraid of what I'll find.

Who are you?

I thought I was Somali or Somali American or American or pues nada.

What does pues nada mean?

Pues nada is a Spanish muletilla, a verbal crutch, something that doesn't necessarily mean anything as such, but is a way of pausing or finishing off a sentence.

You feel like a verbal crutch that doesn't necessarily mean anything as such?

Yes, I feel like an extended pause.

You feel like the end of a sentence?

Yes, but less complete, so I write.

Why do you write?

Not for praise. I don't care about that. It makes me uncomfortable, like money.

Then why?

To discover self? But I'm not comfortable with much of what I discover. It hurts.

You do it for the pain, then?

I don't like pain, I'm already in so much of it, all the time, and my stomach hurts, all the time.

Didn't you do this to yourself, last night, when you binge ate that junk food?

I did, but I made myself forget I was both the cause and victim of my own pain. I don't like it.

Then Why?

Because it's the only thing I've ever known to do. My coffee is getting cold.

Why did you order it if not to drink?

Because I thought I wanted it.

Why do you write if not to make it?

Because I thought I wanted to make it.

So what do you want?

To be happy, to be free of pain.

In this life? Never.

Well, not totally, but you know… At least in less pain than I am now in.

How can you reach that goal?

I hope to write my way out of pain, but so very often, all writing does is bring me more pain.

An endless pain cycle, whether you write or not?

Well, I guess the pain would be there regardless. I guess the writing uncovers things.

And what happens when writing uncovers your pain?

Imagine a cut, a cut that never healed right. Imagine scar tissue atop the cut.

And then?

I use my imagination, with my mush-mouthed words, to try and figure out what caused the cut.

Is that logical?

Commander Tuvok would say no. Because the cut is there, and how it got there is… irrelevant.

Are you Borg now?

Irrelevant. You will comply.

I thought I was making the demands here?

Sorry, I forgot the format. Continue.

Ok. Are you Okay?

Some days I am. Most days, I'm not so sure.

Are you being dramatic?

No, I'm in a lot of pain.

Why not go to the doctor?

I have trust issues. They put me on psych meds before and I'm not going back.

Why don't you just get married?

That's what my parents did and their parents before them and marriage isn't a quick fix.

Damn.

Yeah, I know, I'm sorry, I shouldn't talk about them like that.

Why not?

It's un-Islamic, un-Somali. It's not right. They did the best they could with what they had.

You sound like our old therapist right now.

Yeah, I miss her.

Don't you, tho?

Really do. Never felt so understood. Sometimes I wonder what it would've been like if my parents were therapists. Then again, I've seen children of therapists, and they don't have it figured out, either. Life is a question mark.

Don't you have a new therapist appointment coming up?

Yeah, I do. Brother named _____ . I like his name. And his face, too, looks safe. Reliable.

Doesn't black skin cause you comfort?

Like you wouldn't believe, questioning voice.

Who are you talking to?

I was just about to ask you the same thing.

Why haven't you dropped out of this MFA program yet?

Because **this** is *all* I've ever wanted. At least, that's what I tell people.

*What does **this** mean to you?*

Everything, or so I thought. Well, I mean... Nevermind.

What?

There was that white kid from Kent. Ran into him on The Hill, at that Summit Ave Block Party. It was my first time on that block since I'd gotten (mostly) sober. He saw me and I tried to avoid talking to him, because I knew what he would say, but he was persistent and walked over to me.

> "How you been?"
> "Alright, you?"

After the pleasantries, he asked if I still did spoken word, to which I replied no. It took a while for the words to come to my mouth, feeling like mush as my tongue struggled to wrangle them loose from my voice box. I was on lithium because, after my last major breakdown, the psych ward doctors decided I was bipolar. All they had to go on was my psych ward record because I never did long term outpatient care. I guess it was enough. Anyway, my mind was heavy. Lithium slowed me down something terrible. I hated myself and hoped this would change that for me. I remember my birthday that year, on lithium. I walked to the playground with my little sisters and watched them have a blast. It feels good to be seen by people who don't judge you, who accept you even when you don't accept yourself. A big part of living with childhood trauma is, for me, rejecting the parts of reality I find unpalatable. Sometimes I reject myself. Ole boy kept talking at me.

"So why'd you give up spoken word? You have a gift. The world deserves to hear it."

I've been hearing this for a long time. I don't know what it means for the world to require my gift. Some days, it takes all of my energy just to keep walking. How can I be expected to inspire anyone when all my energy is spent trying to find hope?

"I don't want to talk about it. That writing wsn't for me. I got tired of being a spectacle."

Sensing my unease, the kid from Kent decided to switch subjects. He asked if I remembered chewing on mescaline fish gummies in the living room of that party house. How could I forget, the Seattle rain forever falling against the windowpanes, three in the morning, tripping out to Air's 10,000Hz Legend album. What I couldn't tell him was that the memory, and all the memories like it, were the reason I ended up on meds and hating myself. Or maybe I already hated myself – probably, yeah. Maybe I'm still trying to find ways to wash that hate off of me. Maybe writing is the most effective scrub brush.

Damn, dude.

What I'm trying to say is I couldn't walk away from writing if I tried. I've tried. Like suicide, I've tried. Neither concept ever stuck.

So, if you can't walk away from it, and you can't stomach to do it, are you just fighting yourself?

I guess. Fighting and losing. But what's a conflict-free life for someone who was born in a war?

Yeah, don't I know it. Wait, sorry. I'm supposed to ask questions. What does life mean to you?

You're not doing a very good job of being my therapist.

Who said I was your therapist? I'm just a voice.

My bad, G. Carry on.

Aight. So, where were we?

We were talking about why I can't write, why I can't quit this MFA. How I hurt.

That's heavy stuff, Slim. Who is Slim?

That's the name of an alter-ego character I wrote fiction as.

Where's Slim now?

Not sure, lost track of him. Kinda walked away from Slim.

What did he mean to you?

He was a play on words. Somali, skinny, black hawk down, famine. Lanky with a potbelly like malnourished children. Like the kids they used to show on Feed the Kids infomercials in the mid 90s. The same kids I would get compared to in elementary school like, "Is that your cousin?"

Damn, dude, your family history is complex and full of pain, huh?

You should know, you were there for all of it.

Was I though?

Maybe I'm making you up now as a character who was there with me. A representation for the memories I can't remember. The new Slim, but bodyless.

Was there anyone there with you through all that pain?

My family, yeah. But I felt alone; needed more.

What you mean?

Emotional support.

They didn't provide that for you?

It's a concept that didn't exist in our culture when I was growing up.

Still doesn't?

Still doesn't.

So what does that mean for you and your life?

I guess that's why I write.

To provide emotional support for yourself?

I guess that's right.

You guess?

Nah, I know it.

What would happen if you didn't write?

First, I would fall apart. Then, it'd be like I lost a part of myself to the night.

To the night?

Like a thief ran off with my heart.

A bit melodramatic, don't you think?

I try not to think. Most of my time is spent dissociating.

What does that word mean to you?

To dissociate is to reject reality in favor of staring into the abyss.

What abyss is that? Your life can't be that dark, can it?

You'd be surprised, phantom voice.

Are you evading the question?

Yes and no.

Explain?

A thought came into my mind that I want to explore, but I don't want to abandon our format.

Alright, permission to detour and come back. What's your thought?

I read somewhere that writers who want to make it... Hold on, I'm getting distracted.

Distracted from your distraction?

I wanted to say something but then I started to doubt its veracity.

That's not very productive, is it? Doubt?

In matters of life, art and faith, no. Doubt is the enemy.

Who or what are some of your other enemies?

People that order plain bagels with a shrug and a question mark.

As if they're not sure of what they want?

Exactly. I'm one of those people.

You're your own enemy?

In many ways, yes, and I wish I could defeat myself so this battle would end.

What value does the uncertainty of not knowing what you want carry for you?

It gives me the option to not commit. It helps me stay uncommitted - to life and to writing.

Thought you did this for the love of the writing, bro?

Lol, yeah. So did I.

Then what?

I read somewhere that Nas was finally sick and tired of celebrating Illmatic. I wrote that record 25 years ago, he said. I did another Symphony Orchestra rendition this year, got another plaque for it. It's time to bury it.

Isn't Illmatic a classic?

Sure, but how'd you feel if you produced a body of work spanning decades and people only ever focused on *one* tiny part of that body? And compared everything you did after that to it?

I'd feel sick to my stomach. Weren't you sick to your stomach this morning?

Still am, but I'm not sure if it's a physical sick. I'm trying to write my way out of it.

And you're still nursing that same coffee from an hour ago, aren't you?

I didn't even want coffee, my stomach, but it's part of my ritual. Wake up, reject reality, write.

You're an interesting character, aren't you?

I wish I could write interesting characters, aha ha.

Is that a real laugh or an internet laugh?

It's the kind of laugh that fills the space between reality and dreamscapes.

Like the difference between feeling real and un?

Like the difference between nada y pues nada.

Like you will be the difference?

Like a Jay Dilla Album on repeat at the Faire Gallery Café in 2011, sipping on a Nutella Mocha, scribbling away on poetry notebooks, unemployed as ever, rain never ceasing, corner of Melrose and Olive, around the corner from David the Skater's place, but this was before I met David, and before David moved back to Wisconsin, or Kentucky, or wherever. The remainder is the difference, like the medium is the message, like Dilla grinding out his most essential album on that deathbed of his, making beats with the last of his strength as he felt the shadows closing in on him. Art means different things to different people. For some of us it's a way out, without giving up. Nobody wants to die, just want the pain to ease. And art is a great way of doing that.

These tangents of yours have to stop, you know?

I'm not sure what I know anymore, Phantom Voice.

You've capitalized my name now. Why?

Because I guess you deserve a name, this voice that I'm talking to, inside my head, on this page.

So who am I to you?

Just a voice, I guess. A refraction for my thoughts. A device.

That hurts to hear, Slim.

Don't confuse me with Slim. I'm not Slim. I think you're Slim Evolved, but I'm not Slim.

And I'm not a device. A device is something you use to write. I'm just a Voice.

People who hear voices are said to be crazy, you know.

Is that supposed to be an insult? To me or to you?

Is there even a difference?

Will you be the difference?

Like an agent of change? I'd hope so, deep down. But I don't know if I'm strong enough.

You said something about voices earlier, why didn't you explore it more?

Because I ate a bucket of Chipotle before bed last night and my stomach is doing enough exploring for the both of us.

This seems to be a recurring theme for you: overeat, sleep.

My boy Snax Maui taught me how to gain weight back in HS Football. Eat, go to sleep, repeat.

That doesn't sound very healthy, does it?
Nothing about football is healthy. Nothing about being American is, either.

I like that. America as an unhealthy way of being.

Got a lot of doctors here, most of them unhealthy. They'll tell ya where you got shot, tho.

And flash a light on your corpse?

Whoah, look who's being dark now.

Sorry, I forgot my place.

Nah, you're good for it. Don't sweat.

Is it true that in HS they teased you for how much you sweat?

Yes, especially the football team, who were supposed to be my friends, my protection from social ridicule.

So they caused more harm than good?

Absolutely. Had racist coaches. One of 'em was named _____. Believed in Football, but not God – that's so weird to me. One time he saw a bible on the table and laughed out loud. He shouted, "God has no place in Football!" The hubris of atheists has always unnerved me. He was a stonemason (the trade, not the cult). He walked with a limp, used to play linebacker back in the day. That meant he was violent on the field. Made me wonder how that kind of violence didn't follow a person off the field. Maybe it did. Maybe it was turned inwards. Violence towards one's own soul, manifested as a lack of belief in God.

What kind of violence did football do to you?

Violence to my soul. Ended up choosing between 2-a-day practices and fasting Ramadan.

That's tough, bro. Don't blame yourself, you were only a kid.

Hey, thanks, Voice. I appreciate that.

You're good. I could feel you tensing up, not wanting to write.

Yeah, I don't like talking about HS Football. That stuff really messed me up. But I still watch the NFL on Sundays like it'll save me or sum'n. And Sundays ain't even my holy day, I'm Muslim.

Like how you thought those HS Football players would save you from social ridicule?

You damn skippy, Voice.

I'm not so sure I like that name.

Tough, I think it's already stuck.

Well, you're the writer, you can change it, can't you?

That'd be cheating, like fiction. That's not fair.

Not fair to whom? And didn't 7 of 9 not have any moral qualms about cheating?

She said cheating was irrelevant in the face of reaching a goal. All that mattered was efficiency.

All she ever wanted was perfection.

7 of 9, tertiary adjunct of unimatrix zero-one.

Easily one of your favorite characters in the history of television, right?

So much so. She's got a special place. She meant a lot of things to me at a conflicted time in my life.

Tell me more about that.

I'd rather not. It hurts.

Ok, don't write about the hurt. Write around it.

That's fair, and useful. Ok. I felt like I could relate to her.

A white woman playing half android, half human, separated from a collective to become an individual among a crew of individuals and who possessed no discernible feelings?

She could feel, she just didn't see its value.

So maybe envy is a better word, in place of relate?

Yes, I envied her ability to not feel. I felt too much. Still do.

I feel you bro.

I knew you would.

Right. Tell me about Commander Tuvok.

That was my guy for real. All logic, all smarts, no emotions. Vulcans have highly volatile emotions which, if they go unchecked, consume them whole. So they undergo years of meditation and mental training to help them suppress those emotions. They worship logic. It's really weird. But it works for them, those Vulcans, those imaginary beings.

Seems to be a trend. Another unfeeling character that spoke to you.

I guess when your world is a rush of uncontrollable emotions, you start to see emotionless but functional characters as heroes. You conflate their functionality with a lack of emotionality. You think that if only you were without emotion, maybe you could function. Be whole.

Where most people saw deficiency, you saw perfection.

Like 7 of 9.

Like Commander Tuvok.

The Doctor on *Voyager* was a hologram, but he was more believable than some of the ancillary characters. He sang opera and watched theatre and pronounced it thee-ay-ter. He was bougie.

A three-dimensional projection, a computer simulation, had more emotions than real humans?
Or at least, fictional characters imagined up by real human beings.

What if you could go back in time and be a guest writer for an episode of Star Trek: Discovery?

I'd love that, but, you said *Discovery* instead of *Voyager.*

It's all Star Trek, isn't it?

No, it's different story-lines in the same character universe.

Bro, you're such a nerd. No wonder they gave you a hard time in the hood.

No hood passes for allegedly white-talking black boys in the hood.

True. Wasn't there a time when you lived in the hood and a friend of yours read your essay?

Yeah, _____, who was Eritrean. Gave me a ride to school every day. I found allies where I could.

What was his reaction when he read that essay of yours?

He said, "You write how a white man talks," or something to that effect.
What did that do to you?

Tore me up something terrible. Like post-binge stomach pain.

What do you say now about people giving you critique and feedback on your writing?

I tell 'em I'm not interested, don't trust their intentions.

Or their care with your words?

Their lack of care.

What did _____'s response to your essay really do to you?

Man it broke me in a way that I can't explain. He was supposed to be my friend. I didn't have any Somali friends cuz I grew up so isolated, and the few Somali kids at school were more Somali than American, and I didn't fit in with them, so _____ became a close-enough stand-in. Another son of East African immigrants raised in America, going to school in the ghetto proper, just like me. He was Christian where I was Muslim, but he was not quite Black American, so we could relate on a lot of things. You gotta find reflections of yourself however you can to survive this country.

You write a lot about surviving this country, surviving HS, surviving, full stop. What does it mean for you to survive?
To write, to pray, to avoid my family sometimes.

Ouch, that's hard to hear bro.

Even harder to feel.

Makes you wish you were 7 of 9.

Except male.

Commander Tuvok.

Except pale.

You don't mean that.

I don't, lol, I'd never want to be white, but it rhymed.

Who else did you find parts of yourself in?

Commander Chakotay, with the face tattoos. Belana Torres: half-human, half-Klingon, all conflicted.

You really know these characters inside and out.

They were my home away from home, every day when I came home. My escape button.

What channel did it used to come on?

Q13 Fox, every night. 11PM. Even on school nights.

Did it start at 11 or end at 11?

Not sure, but I know 11 was involved. And I know this was before the time of streaming WiFi, so if a show came on TV, you had to know exactly what time and day it aired. And you waited in anticipation. Boy, I had whole entire channel lineups memorized.

And you say you have a hard time memorizing.

It's selective memory. I remember the things which carry emotional meaning for me.

You're an emotional guy.

It's how I see the world. Some people see it through images. Others in words. Still others in story.
Tell me about the power of story?

I'm not sure if I'm best equipped to do that.

Didn't you just teach an undergraduate class three weeks of fiction?

I sure tried.

And before that three weeks of poetry?

Again, tried.

Tell me what poetry means to you?

More than it does to people who call themselves poets.

Wear a tight shirt and call yourself a poet, then.

It would steal the light of poetry from me, if I did that.

You have an interesting way of staging sentences.

That's an interestingly staged sentence, Voice.

Makes you wonder if we're not the same person.

Ain't tryna think about that, fam.

It's probably for the best that you don't.

Anyway.

Yeah?

Talk to me about Atlanta.

The questioned becomes the questioner.

Just vibe with me for a second.

Alright. I remember Country Time Lemonade mix in the plastic tub with the giant twist-off cap.

What else?

An 80s station wagon with the wood paneling on the outside.

Who owned it?

An old white lady that was devoutly Christian but helped new immigrants of different faiths.

Think she was tryna convert y'all?

Maybe. Maybe she did it for the sake of God. Maybe she was Borg.

How did mom feel about her?

I remember Hooyo saying, "She's such a good person, if only she were Muslim."

What did she mean by that?

That you can only go to heaven if you're Muslim, and as Muslims, we believe…

Why'd you stop?

I feel like I'm explaining something I don't need to.

We can switch gears if you like, no worries.

Appreciate you bro.

We all we got.

I know that's right.

ATL, tho.

First night we landed from Africa, it was a drive-by on our block in Decatur, GA.

Aha, ha.

It is kinda funny, isn't it?

Yeah, like, "We left Africa for THIS?"

Boy, they didn't tell us in Africa about the cost of being blessed with Black skin in America.

Would you have still come if they did?
Well, I was only 7 when we got here. I didn't have a choice.

Kids are so precious.

Innocence intact.

World ain't robbed em of it yet.

Sometimes I wonder.

What it is you wonder, bro?

If we'd (I'd) grown up in ATL instead of SEA.

Think we'd have a country accent?

Definitely wouldn't sound white.

That's a hurtful and ignorant thing to say, bro.

I think what _____ meant when he said it was: "You are incapable of producing vocal and dialectical patterns congruent with the African American Orthodox Language."
What does that even mean?

*Basically, he was accusing me of being white- washed, because I didn't seem Black, as in: not culturally competent in the African American experience. That's a wild concept because I didn't grow up in an African American household, I grew up in an African Immigrant household. I never considered that my skin color made me different until I got here because, for the first 7 years of my life, everyone in the world looked just like me. My world was Black, so I didn't know what it meant to be Black outside of that. Or what it meant to be or **sound** Black in America. And I didn't know that sounding Black was a codified language which protected Black lives in a hostile white country. I didn't have access to any of that information in high school, and I barely can make sense of it now in graduate school. I didn't know I was supposed to sound anything.*

How does one even sound black?

AAVE. Ebonics. The way that some Black people speak, and by Black I mean African American, my cousins who were stolen from our continent, who survived generational genocide & paid for our (African immigrants') right to be here with their bodies, with loss of agency to those bodies, who held onto their native cultures and rebirthed those cultures in a way that let them survive in this hellhole of a country; whose spirits wouldn't let them break, and let them become what they are today, which is something more beautiful than I have words to say.

I think it was Kemba (rapper, not baller) who said: this came from love // we made a civilization from mud // we made a culture to break out the hood

I have so much love and respect for my brothers, sisters, cousins in this American struggle.

Wish all our people saw it that way, huh?

Wish they didn't believe what the white man say.

Wish they didn't read your writing and say: you sound like a white man, Said.

Some things just don't leave you.

We call that Trauma, bro.

Believe me, I know. Hey.

What?

Let's switch back, I'm hurting talking about this. I'm not as strong as you.

My bad lil bro. I'll take over now. Or should we take a break?

I think I'd like that.

Alright. I'll get up with you on the other side.

Say less.

Stay blessed.

I can attest to the fact that Mohamed Shaiye and Safia Jama are the parents of Said, Liban and Abdirizak Farah because Mohamed Shaiye is my brother. I was present at their wedding in 1986 in Mogadishu Somalia. I knew Safia Jama before she was married to my brother also.

At the time that Said was born we were all still living in Mogadishu Somalia. I worked in the hospital where Said was born and I was working at the time that my sister-in-law came in to have Said. I came to visit when the baby was born. After the baby was born, I bought some baby clothes and helped clean my sister-in-law's house. I helped prepare the house for the mother and the new baby.

I lived in Nairobi during the time that Liban was born. Liban was born in the refugee camp in Liboi, Kenya. My brother called to tell us that the new baby was born. It was hard to travel and visit in Kenya because we were refugees there but we were often in contact by phone and letters during the time we were living in Kenya. We sent gifts of clothes for the new baby.

I lived in the United States when Abdirizak was born. My brother called to say the new baby was born and we sent money for the family. We talked on the phone regularly during the times that we were separated and I was in the United States.

I came to United States in 1992 and my brother came with his family in 1995. I went to visit them in Georgia when they first came. We both moved to and now live in Seattle and our families are close to each other.

$*$ $*$ $*$

Say bro.

Yeah?

I'm ready to continue, now.

Let's get it. What you tryna talk about?

I'm not sure. Been stressing about this project.

What project that is?

This one I have to write for brother Doug's class.

What's he asking of you?

Wants me to pinpoint how I'm going to write a cross-genre hybrid thing.

What does that even mean?

Hell if I know. Something experimental, quote/unquote.

Air quotes for the win, tho.

Al Gore smoking endo.

You call it Endo, but it smell like out doe.

Look man, you didn't even pay for this. Lol. Friday is forever *that* flicc.

Tell me about an experience you had watching that movie?

Ok. Gasworks park, overlooking Lake Union. I want to say it was a Friday night.

Who were you with?

M. She spelled her name with exactly ten n's on AOL Instant Messenger.

That AIM, tho.

I had no aim or ambition at that time. I think this was late 2007. Shortly before I dropped out.

UW really messed you up, huh?

Can't even go into all that, breh.

Alright, happy thoughts, think happy thoughts. What was so special about that Friday night?

We were both rolling, hard. Took a blue dolphin each. That means ecstasy, for the uninitiated. We were laughing, smoking. Watching Friday on my portable DVD player. I still remember that scene like it was last Friday. Never wanted it to end.

You used to smoke a ton of reefer, huh?

Yeah, it was really hard to quit. People kept telling me it wasn't *physically addicting.*

But you didn't smoke it for physical reasons, did you?

Nah, it was lack of spirit. Lack of faith. Tryna fill a void. Tryna patch over my missing-ness.

How did that work out for you?

Not too well, lol.

I believe it. Ok, then what happened?

See, M was this girl I had a crush on. But she didn't like me. She was into white boys. She was Viet, and I grew up in White Center with crushes on all the Viet girls in my honors classes. I was around them all the time, and they had the weirdest senses of humor, and that really did it for me, and I was really lonely, you know? Common theme in my life.

So M was like a college version of everything you wished you could have had in high school?

Yeah, a simulacrum of all my old Viet crushes. And so, history repeats itself, you know, she wasn't feeling a brother like that. Told me I was a *good friend.*

Good grief. You poor sucker. So much rejection.

Don't I know it. So I'd send her messages, hoping to be validated, hoping she'd respond, hoping we dated.

But you're Muslim, you're not supposed to be doing any of that stuff before marriage.

I wasn't the most practicing brother back then, if you couldn't tell by the gratuitous drug use.

Fair enough, we been through a lot. Just make sure you repent.

May Allah forgive me, and may He keep me coming back to Him in humble submission.

So what ended up happening with you and M?

A whole lot of damn nothing. Crazy story: one time she invited me to a house party in Tacoma. Tacoma has always been a whack version of Seattle. This is a bad memory. I don't actually want to talk about it.

Fair enough, big bro, you good for it.

Appreciate you, man.

What is family for?

Misunderstandings, mostly.

Lol, funny guy.

I try.

Ok. Why do you love that movie so much, Friday? Why do movies and shows entrance you?

They're these perfect disappearance devices, you know? Way better than a book of fiction; less work to fall into. It's real people with emotions and faces and cinematography and background scores and cut scenes and… it's so compelling, when done right.

Yeah, you ever thought of making movies?

Against my religion.

But you watch them?

I shouldn't be doing that, either. Waste a lot of time and implant subliminal messages.

Hmmm. So what is this?

Shhhh. You ask the wrong questions sometimes.

UNITED STATES DEPARTMENT OF JUSTICE
IMMIGRATION AND NATURALIZATION SERVICE

Refugee Application for Permanent Residence S

INSPECTION UNDER PL 96-211 CRITERIA

ENTERED Sep 27, 1995 _____ ✓ Sec. 209(a) RE
(Date)

Supporting Documents	Rec'd	Need	MISS
Medical	MAR 13 1998		ON
FD-258	WAIVER/CHILD		MARITAL S CITY OF E
Photographs	NOV 08 1997		LAST COUN MOTHER'S
G-325		X	FATHER'S ADMISSION
I-590	✓		INTERVIEW(S)
I-643	NOV 08 1997		(1) _____
I-94	NOV 08 1997		(2) _____

✳ ✳ ✳

And we back.

How long's it been?

A day or two, who knows?

That's real.

Tell me how you feel?

Like throwing up.

What's wrong now?

Ate too much Dominoes. Medium pizza and 8-piece cinnamon bread twists with icing.

What was it this time?

The reason I ate the Dominoes?

Yeah, I know it wasn't just hunger.

It was, but not that kind of hunger.

How many kinds of hunger are there?

It depends. Soul hunger. Heart hunger. Identity hunger. So much hunger.

Ok, what caused this particular hunger for you?

Some stuff happened last night, it was hard.

Breathe.

Ok.

I see you let your stomach go, you were clutching it, spasming.

Ain't even realize.

Feel your heartbeat.

Okay.

Breathe from the diaphragm.

I am.

Did you spell diaphragm right?

I did. I mean, you did.

We did.

Sho nuff.

Like kiss my converse? Like Dub Cee's Verse in Bow Down?

West Side Connect Gang, Connect Gang.

B-B-Bang.

What does that even mean?

Who knows what artists mean when they say things?

Not even the artists themselves, half the time.

Tap your feet and pick up what I'm putting down.

I thought you gave up rap?

I did. But I still move. Maneuver.

Bop of the head as you type, huh?

Reason why these bars seem to have a flow to em.

It's always funny when white people talk about flow in writing and they've never hit a flow.

Never coasted to a beat, have they?

Never been in a mosh pit, half of them.

Never wrote in the studio to an instrumental and then gave it up because they realized words are hard to confine a rhythm to.

Not to say that rappers don't write hot 16s to instrumentals.

I feel like you're avoiding something.

Lol, obviously. Reason why I'm talking sideways about nothing.

What's got you?

I had to sit at a table for two hours with a group of people and two… no one of those people…

I see your tensing up again. This isn't worth writing about.

You right. Let's switch topics.

What else is there to talk about?

The weird tension in a room when I walk into it.

*Bro, you're **avoiding** something.*

Who says I have to confront it?

Because you can't move on if you don't. Was it that phone call from _____?

Yes.

You must address it, young.

I'm good. I make the rules here, not you. I'll avoid anything I want to avoid.

Fair enough, it's your world.

The World Is Yours, Chico, And Everything In It. So Say Goodnight To The Bad Guy.

I can attest to the fact that Mohamed Shaiye and Safia Jama are the parents of Said, Liban and Abdirizak Farah because Safia Jama is my sister. I was present at their wedding in 1986 in Mogadishu Somalia.

We were all still living in Mogadishu at the time that Said was born. He was born in Banadir Hospital during the daytime. We received a call to let us know that my sister was in the hospital and I went to visit at the hospital when my sister was there with the new baby. All of us brothers and sisters visited her at the hospital and went to visit her home also. We brought gifts to the hospital and to her home.

Liban was born in Liboi Refugee Camp in Kenya. We all left Mogadishu and fled to Kenya. Here we found each other in the Refugee Camp. Liban was born in the small hospital in the camp. I followed my sister when she went to the hospital to have the new baby and saw the new baby very early. We did not have so much for gifts and things at this time because life was difficult in the refugee camp.

Abdirizak was also born in Liboi Refugee Camp, in the hospital in the camp. Someone came to me and told me that Safia was in labor and I went to visit her in the hospital. Some of our other brothers and sisters were also living in Liboi Refugee Camp and were there when Liban and Abdirizak were born. It was the same as with Liban, we did not have much to give for gifts.

My sister came to America in 1995 and I came to America in 1999. I first came to Georgia where my mother and some of my brothers and sisters. Later I came to Seattle. When I came to Seattle I met up with my sister and her family here. Now we are neighbors.

Say bro.

How you been, man?

I can't call it. You know how it is out here.

I really do, tho. It's been a few days, huh?

Yeah, not sure what's been keeping me from continuing this project.

Heard you been doing a lot of reading?

A lot of avoiding, really. Disappearing into my books and finding more books to eat.

Feeding the mind is a worthy endeavor, young.

Yeah, you're right. I think I found a new best friend.

What happened to your old best friend?

I'm not sure if I had one. I forgot him. A patchwork of best friends keep me floating.

That's interesting.

Or cowardice, idk. I've grown tired of this book.

You've said that before. Why?

I don't know, I guess I thought this would be a great way to avoid facing the pain of my past.

Thought that trauma could be diverted with a clever call-and-response format?

Yeah, I guess.

You sure guess a lot for someone who seems to know a lot.

I don't like to brag. I'm more comfortable with seeming aloof and unsure of myself.

Who's your favorite rapper?

Of all time? Probably Lil Wayne. Nacho Picasso. Das Racist.

I asked you for one.

Who can choose one rapper, one book, one best friend?

What excites you in life right now?

Freedom of time. The time to write, or to tell people that I'm writing.

You're not that busy, are you?

It's not about me. What are we doing here?

Nothing serious. Tell me about your past.

There's a lot to tell. A lot of vignettes. I don't know how I'll write this memoir.

Is this not memoir?

I don't know what this is, but there's too much space to call it memoir. I don't know what I am sometimes. There's too much space to call me a person.

Hard to write about yourself when your sense of self is always moving, isn't it?

I just write another sentence, check out another book about living with childhood trauma.

Tell me about Kierkegaard.

I couldn't tell you much more than he was dark as hell. I mean, dark. And, also, he reminds me of a girl.

Of a girl?

I can't even say her name, but she was Danish. Somali, but Danish. Thought I'd marry her.

How many times have you almost married a girl?

I'm not sure if I've ever gotten close to marrying a girl. I've said it, though.

Words don't mean the same when you don't go through with them.

Words keep me safe, keep me dreaming perfect dreams, when life feels so imperfect.

I know you don't mean life itself is imperfect.

I mean my understanding of it.

Well, you don't know everything, so of course your view is limited.

Just like my life span, which grows shorter by the day, but at least I'm doing what I love.

At least you're writing, sipping tea, chugging coffee expeditiously.

I be on my grizzly, bro. On my grind time.

Tryna shine, right?

Like Vince Staples in 2014.

Shyne Coldchain Vol. 2?

That was my album, for real. It's hard to make a distinction between "journal writing" and writing to change the world.

What does that even mean?

I guess I assume people think my writing is diary, so it can't be "literary," or whatever.

You spend entirely too much time thinking about what people think about you and your writing.

I can't help it, born like this.

Like Bukowski said.

I used to look up (& down) to him.

That was a dark time in your life, huh?

That's a common theme of my life, huh.

Yuh-huh.

I'm going to switch over to my other document and work some stuff out.

Why don't you just do it here?

It would break the pattern of what we have going and I don't want to lose another best friend.

Fair. Take your time. Come back whenever.

That's why I appreciate you, see.

Say less, G.

My Sheikh has been trying to reach me and I've kept a steady distance. I don't know man. It's so easy for me to feel betrayed by people. *Who are these people you're talking about?* I'm not even sure. I ask myself questions that I can't answer. *And you hope for the answers to present themselves in the form of new questions?* Or something like it. I think I'm forgetting what writing means to me, but I forget that on the daily, and then I remember it. *I – I mean, you – keep thinking that what you're writing is not worth anything.* Well, yes, I wouldn't keep writing if I didn't. *So you write from a place of fear?* It's a hell of a motivator, yeah. *That's macabre.* Different people need to be engaged with the process in different ways. *Isn't it time to go pray?* It is time to go pray.

Who are you talking to, Slim? Myself and the second voice in my writing, which I'm still not sure where it's coming from, or what it represents, or who it is. *Aren't you the only one here?* Yeah, sure, why not. *So, then, this second voice is just a reflection of your shadow thoughts.* I don't know if it's that easy. *Explain?* I mean I don't think this is a part of me, but clearly I'm writing your voice, so it must be. *So, then, who are you?* If I knew that, I wouldn't be writing. *Isn't that selfish?* No, because who I am is a representation of who my people are, and my people are suffering. *Struggling?* Juggling life between rafts and the sea.

My guy.

What up doe?

Just thinking about Blink 182.

What song?

Carousel. The extended intro guitar riff. It feels so melodic, like another world. They were such a good escape for me.

Those were hard times, needed something a little bit wrong, a little bit sinful, to keep you going.

Funny how that works. I never know what keeps me moving until I need to be moved.

I think you're struggling with something today.

I'm supposed to warm up to that, what you breaking the mold for?

I can feel it in your left shoulder.

Call it the weight of the world, of these books in my bag slung across a shoulder.

Like how the cool kids in middle school, 2001, wore the one-strap Jansports across the belly.

They were so cool, or, at least they thought they were. And I was so jealous.

Remember that time…

In middle school, I think it was the English teacher's class who went to Iowa State.

Yeah, the one whom you unleashed a racist rant on her Facebook a few years ago.

Anti-racist rant. I accused her of being a white liberal woman, told her she *was* the problem, not just a part of it, and that she had no business teaching black kids to hate themselves in the hood.

Boy, school really did a number on you.

This country tap-dances on me still.

They talk of racial progress as if it's a thing of the past.

As if I can't hardly breathe right now.

So what's really on your mind?

Can't get decent sleep at night. I see mattress commercials on the sides of buses and wonder if that's my problem.

Do you even have a problem?

At least 99, but Jay-Z ain't one.

Tell me about the Black Album.

Came out in middle school, when I used to hang out at the boys and girls club, Park Lake Homes Site 2. Asian brother named W was the manager there, so he became our unofficial mentor. Asian dudes from the hood always had so much swag.

They had that social mobility, plus the viscerality of hood life.

They could move in and out of social classes with ease.

While you were (are) trapped by your skin.

I just want to publish everything I write, right after I write it, before I have a chance to second guess it.

Tell me about the Black Album.

Came out in 2002, I think, in middle school, and W used to listen to it. Well, everyone did. We'd play HALO on original XBOX and talked of how cutting edge it was. W would be in the background, cooking Turkey Tetrazzini for us as he talked with someone about Elton Brand's viability as an NBA player. I'd sneak off into a quiet, dark room to listen to that album, or some other album, probably Blink 182.

So you went to the B&G Club to escape your home life, and then you escaped the escape by going into a separate room. An escape room of sorts.

This was before I discovered writing. I wish I'd started writing sooner. It was always too loud to write, tho.

Is that why you encourage so many Somali kids to start writing?

Absolutely. It's a lonely road I'm on, trying to make a writer out of myself in a world that doesn't require or desire it of me, but I want them to have the tools to be okay with themselves.

So they don't have to walk into dark rooms at boys and girls clubs across the country?

Hoping no one walks in and catches them listening to pop-punk emo heartbreak songs in the middle of the hood, where the only thing you're allowed to listen to is *gangsta*.

Tell me about expected and assumed renditions of Blackness in the hood?

That's a stupid question.

Why do you say that?

Because the girl(s) I had a crush(es) on (all) listened to P.Diddy and Kube 93 while I went onto Limewire and pirated (it's in my blood to pirate) Blink-182 songs. I tried to share my love of the songs with them on AIM. They were like, nah dude, my favorite song right now is *Let's Get Married P.2*.

What a twisted web you found yourself in.

I've felt sticky my whole life.

In how many ways?

More than I care to count.

More than you can count?

More than I can care to think about.

So now you're here. Purple Haze, the album.

Ironic that I used to listen to Hendrix's Purple Haze, getting drunk with white boy's in Federal Way. Then I changed and listened to Cam'ron's Purple Haze, getting drunk with white girls on The Hill. I wonder why I hung out with so many white people.

What's ironic about alcoholism?

Nothing, unless you've managed to beat it. And everything, because it's against my religion.

Tell me about a time you used "that's against my religion" to get out of something.

Just last night, actually.

What was the thing?

I'd rather not say, but it had to do with school.

Was your reasoning valid?

Oh, yeah. The thing was definitely against my religion, in every way.

Tell me about the term "Muslim For Clout."

A friend of mine coined it. Refers to people who claim Muslim identity out of political convenience, to seem more oppressed than the next man in line, in this liberal representational identity politics nation.

That seems counterproductive; isn't Islam one of the most marginalized identities in the world?

Absolutely, people are being tortured and detained around the world for it. Gitmo, Burma, Uyghur China.

So why would anyone claim to be Muslim if they didn't believe in or act according to its principals?

We live in a confusing time where "truth" isn't deemed important. It's like… like… like watching a building burn and all the occupants are smiling, saying what burning building?

What burning, indeed. Melting faces with grimaces shouldn't be confused for smiles. Tell me about writing.

I write to save my life.

Tell me about praying.

I pray to save my soul.

Tell me about Umrah.

I wish and hope I could (can) go every year, Insha Allah.

Tell me about recovery.

I don't think of it. I used to be addicted to substances, now I'm not. People look at me like I have a magical answer or cure for the addiction problem. Nah, dude, I went through it and now I'm here, Alhamdulillah.

Surely you must have some insights, tho?

Sure, but I think people confuse that with a roadmap to sobriety. I don't have all (or any) of the answers.

Tell me about helping others.

It's a part of me. It's how I was raised. It's my foundation.

Tell me about helping yourself.

I don't think of it as much as I should. A part of me sees it as selfishness.

Tell me about a friend named Wesley.

Wesley Skye. The homie from middle and high school.

How'd y'all meet?

In track, 8th grade, I think. Or was it 7th? Or was it 10th?

You have a funny memory, friend.

Funny thing is, I believe my memory is intact, except for the places where there're glaring holes.

Tell me about editing your writing.

I don't have a problem with it, per se, but I hate for white people to do it.

Some would call you racist, the way you talk about white folks.

If anyone calls me a racist, I bet they're not Black.

Have you ever had a Black editor?

I can't recall.

That might be your problem, Slim.

One of many.

Seven of Nine.

We are Borg. Prepare for assimilation. Resistance is futile.

Say bro.

What up doe.

Got something on my mind.

What that is?

Thinking about some of our old crushes.

Fantasizing?

Maybe, but like, reminiscing.

Ok, name one.

Natalie.

The first one that got away, huh?

Yeah, but I don't want to write about her getting away. I want to describe the possibility of her.

That's fair, Voice. I saw her profile on Facebook the other day.

She has a kid now.

Life is crazy, huh?

Couldn't have been with her even if I could.

No sex before marriage, we Muslim bro.

We human, bro.

Not to say that being Muslim is being inhuman.

But to say that being Muslim requires a lot of self-discipline, for the sake of Allah.

We give up a lot of the pleasures of this life for the hope of being rewarded in both lives.

They don't get that we sacrifice temporary pleasures for endless pleasures, for the hope of pleasing our God.

And there is a lot of pleasure to be had in that, isn't there?

Well, yeah. It's Faith manifested. A core tenet of Islam is belief in the unseen.

We can't see the fruits of our labor, but we believe. And that makes our belief stronger.

There are times when holding onto your faith is like holding onto a burning coal.

The devil, sometimes, grabs you with a grip unceasing.

And sometimes I feel like I could never go astray.

And the devil has different ways of grabbing hold. Over-confidence is one such way.

I realize that I haven't said anything about that crush of mine.

If you'll allow me, I think I know why.

Why that is?

You're afraid of the implications.

Nonsense. I'm human, I have needs.

1, Are you, tho? 2, Those needs – you won't get them fulfilled moving how you do.

That's a whole lotta judgement in one statement, Slim.

Look, I'm sorry, I don't mean to come across like a typical *Soomaal.*

Then what?

Picture this: you are 7 of 9.

Easy enough, minus the whole white woman thing.

Right, we're Black, and men at that. Picture yourself as a person with the same traits and name as 7 of 9, and nothing more.

Done.

You're standing on the bridge of the ship. No, scratch that – you're in the Captain's ready room.

It's 2 AM.

She has a book open by the fireside and is drinking freshly replicated coffee, black. But she claims she's –

Not interested in a philosophical discussion about individuality at 2 AM?

Exactly. She's probably reading poetry, or even worse – philosophy.

At 2AM in her ready room, not asleep, having a ship to run, sipping coffee, claiming to be tired.

OK, now I want you to listen to this monologue of 7's, it's fascinating:

"It is unsettling. You say that I am a human being, and yet I am also Borg. Part of me not unlike your replicator. Not unlike the doctor. Will you one day choose to abandon me, as well? I have always looked to you as my example. My guide to humanity. Perhaps I have been mistaken. Goodnight."

You say that I am a human being.

And yet I'm also Said.

Part of me a writer, not unlike a replicator, creating synthetic items for human consumption.

Not unlike the doctor, who Captain Janeway is denying agency in this episode by constantly re-writing his memory files to prevent him from running into a moral dilemma – one of feeling guilt for choosing to save one crew member over the other, and recognizing that he didn't do it out of probability, but out of affection. He chose to save the crewmember that's closer to his heart. And as a result, the other one died. And now he's questioning his individuality, his sanity, his humanity – even though he's a Holographic program, albeit one who's exceeded his program limitations and developed a personality outside his pre-installed parameters.

Not unlike you. Or us. Or whatever.

A young boy who is said to be human, but who is also part of the collective.

You are the collective Said. And Somali people are your Borg.

My old collective, that I've escaped from, and tried to go back to, but realized that I'm too foreign for their systems now. Always have been.

And you still have your Faith to guide you, and shades of cultural tradition to inform you. Your Starfleet, your USS Voyager.

I'm not Somali, I'm something different now. Always have been.

Like when Wesley Skye asked you in 8th grade whether your thought-language was English or Somali.

And how I stopped dead in my tracks, on the Evergreen High red dirt track that reminded me so much of the red dirt of my upbringing, although I couldn't have known it at the time, I'd have to go back to Africa to see the connection, but subconsciously it felt like home, and so when I signed up for Track and Field, I was really just recreating my childhood, running on red dirt, running from an unseen enemy.

Remember that time you edited the scholarship essay for a Somali sister in Dubai?

Yeah, in it she talked about escaping Somalia during the civil war, how her family went north when my family went south. How she was young enough to think it was a vacation, but old enough to remember.

Think of those two sets of parents – hers and yours – how they were forced to make a decision.

Not unlike the doctor, choosing which path to take, which life to save.

Go north, try to start a new life and hope the country got better.

Go south, try to make it to Kenya, knowing there was a higher chance of death, knowing they'd likely not be able to come back.

Wanna talk about moral dilemma? Imagine if your parents made the opposite decision and you ended up growing up in Somalia, in the Arab countries. Or if one your siblings didn't make it for whatever reason.

Well, as Muslims, we have Qadr of Allah to protect us from endless what-if statements, a known playground for the devil and his tactics. But if I were to play along, just hypothetically, I'd say that it would have ate them up in ways I can't imagine.

They always said to you – what was it they said?

"You won't ever understand what it's like to have kids until you have kids."

You can't possibly understand the decisions we had to make in the middle of a war, only thinking of your survival.

"And so how could you be upset with us about what he had to do, when we risked everything for you?"

How could you complain about not having the emotional support you needed when we supported you in every way we knew how?

"How could you not remember that we turned your face away from seeing as much violence as we could, on that long, dark road to Kenya. To America."

You know, life is crazy. There's so much we have to grapple with.

So much we're still coming to terms with.

Not unlike 7 of 9, coming to terms with her humanity.

Trying to understand it.

Ok, I feel you slowing down, this took a dark and unexpected turn. It's time to ease off.

The more I think of it, the more I see you as a guide to keep me protected from danger. You're my Doctor from Voyager.

Maybe I really am the instinctive part of you that took over when you dissociated emotionally, to forget physically, when things got traumatic for you as a child. As a man. As a child expected to be a man.

I'm really vibing with that idea. A Voice; a safety mechanism. The Doctor.

Look, I'm here for you, man. I got your back, sides, and front.

You my niggaa doe!

Like that nigga Roe.

Roedeeziac, the legend!

Best QB / LB to ever walk through Evergreen High School.

And the nicest guy to ever do it, too. Always showed me love.

Remember when you saw him years after HS?

He was a bouncer at a club in Belltown.

I think it was the night you were stupid drunk and thought it was a good idea to shake that cop's hand in the middle of the street.

That racist pig just stood there cross-armed and said, "I don't shake hands on duty."

I think what he meant was, "I don't shake hands with niggers."

Read last night in SIR, by Kenyatta A.C. Hinkle, about how the white cashiers in Louisville, Kentucky avoid touching Black people's hands when they are due change.

As if Blackness is a disease that'll leap off my body and onto yours, whitey. As if we don't deserve change, financial or otherwise.

As if white men don't have a predilection for protecting white women from Black men.

While at the same time creating this sick view of the Black body as nothing more than a sexual device and projecting fear of the imaginary hypersexuality of Black bodies onto their own.

Like we're all just walking phalluses and pectorals and mammories and thighs and hips and…

Anyway, back to the subject. This is dark and disgusting stuff, delving into white psychoses.

Right, back to Roedeezy. I ran up on him that night, but he didn't immediately recognize me.

Probably shocked that you were in a club, alcohol on your breath.

Last he saw me, I was Muslim.

Faith is hard to hang onto in a place like America. In a place that hates so efficiently.

Right, so, you know, Roedeezy was standing there looking like he hadn't aged a day.

What'd you ask him?

Asked what he did after he went to college on a football scholarship.

The hood dream, right?

It was mine too, convinced I wanted the same dream as my peers.

Bro, you can't even ball. Name a sport, you're trash.

Laugh emoji. Slow as hell, bro.

So what did Roe say?

Said he joined up with the Marines after finishing school.

Those Poly Usos were really big on warrior stuff. Football, Marines, Faith.

They really stuck to their guns on that. Big part of the culture. They have big hearts, too, tho.

Samoans showed us a lot of luv in White Center.

A lot of hate, too, tho.

People are multidimensional.

Not unlike 7 of 9.

So what did Roe do in the Marines?

He told me he'd been stationed in Djibouti, which is close enough to Somalia to be Somalia.

But it used to be Somalia, right?

Yeah, before the French ripped it off like a bite out of crime.

Now all the people there speak French and a northern accent of Somali.

I used to see them drive down to Borama every summer when it got too hot in Djibouti.

So what was it like seeing one of your heroes in high school as an adult?

It was surreal. I really looked up to him. He was popular, but a man of faith, and somehow his preaching didn't take away from his popularity. He was strong but sensitive. He was liked by all, always had a smile. He looked out for me and never judged me for being Other than the norm (in a school that was nothing but different types of Other).

Isn't it weird that he was stationed somewhere your people call home?

Does anyone know anything until it passes them by?

Nah, can't say they do. But it ain't been that long since they had niggas in the Bronx Zoo. Ota Benga.

Something on your mind, Slim?

Watched this YouTube video the other day. Types of Black accents in different American Hoods.

That sounds interesting, what'd you notice?

Was watching the young brothers get interviewed by another brother behind the camera. As they talked, with all types of twang and flavor, shouts to their heritage, I noticed how they all looked off into the distance, as if scanning for some unseen enemy.

That's normal in the hood. Didn't you do the same thing growing up?

Yeah, and I didn't think much of it until I read this comment:

Anika A — 5 days ago — 2K Likes

When you're constantly scanning the environment like that, it's called

hypervigilance.

That's trauma in action.

Cover Sheet

Record of Proceeding

NOTE: This is a permanent record of U. S. Citizenship and Immigration Services.

Instructions

$*\ *\ *$

Naomi Wildman.

Explain.

I'm having a gas coughing fit. Feel like throwing up. Clogged up. Can barely breathe.

Boy, that Mankato trip really messed you up, huh?

Sure, but it was more like… what I did to myself to get there and after.

Bodily self-injury. Cutting without the cutting.

Over consumption of all the worst things.

Now you're sitting there, bloated, stomach full of all types of wrong.

Feel physically as bad as I felt emotionally today.

Family is hard.

The hardest.

You keep saying you love them. And you do.

But being around them hurts, too.

That's trauma in action.

May God forgive me.

I love you bro.

I'm sending it right back.

We gone be straight.

Just gotta breathe.

Put on some Voyager.

Let 7 of 9's emotionless voice help you figure it out.

Drift off to the sounds of the end credit theme song.

Dream of the holodeck doors opening and closing

Dream of finding a wholeness within that doesn't come with strings attached.

Dream of providing for yourself what you were never able to get from without.

From external sources.

Naomi Wildman.

Explain.

✳ ✳ ✳

Say bruh.

What it do, baby?

Out here in class again. Reflecting. Killing it.

Oh you're teaching nonfiction to your students, aren't you?

You know it. I'm geeked.

White boys might say stoked.

Don't call me white tho.

Remember the Andy Milonaikais show?

That was one crazy white boy.

Yeah, he was like the forefront of meme culture before meme culture was a culture.

Trippy, I'm thinking of something else.

What that is?

How I'm using my position as a teacher of creative writing in a subversive way.

Shoving Black knowledge down white people's throats, huh?

Trying, to the best of my ability, although shoving might not be the best choice of words.

What would be?

Writing. I remember dreaming about this day on so many nights.

So alone, so afraid.

So, so def (welcome to Atlanta where the players play).

On the dance floor, Evergreen Lunchroom, homecoming dance, 2002 the football team huddled, white boy doing the C-Walk.

I always wondered how he got away with something like that. He seemed more *Black*-Black than me.

Me, the person with actual black skin.

He talked more Blackly than I did, too.

Me, the person from an actual Black continent.

Makes me wonder what exactly Blackness is supposed to mean.

Black me, the person with all the questions, no answers.

Makes me wonder what it all really means.

Me, the person who listens to the same two Kanye albums on repeat.

Makes me wonder what it means to find my dreams.

Come True?

All the way.

Say Alhamdulillah, thank God in your heart, and with your words, and live a life fulfilled.

Gratitude is so necessary to keep walking this line.

And slowing down your breathing is all about recognizing the time.

Time on my mind.

Time on the grind.

I did something new this time, this morning.

What?

Decided to pray in my room instead of going back to sleep.

Instead of braving the cold winds to make it to Masjid?

Instead of not being able to go back to sleep later.

You feel rested then?

And fulfilled. Heart full.

That's amazing bro.

That's love bro.

You already know.

God bless you.

* * *

Boy say.

What that boy say?

Say, how'd you survive yesterday?

By the grace of Allah, really.

St. Cloud is a racist place, huh?

More than I knew.

More than you could say?

More than I allowed my body to say.

More than they can sentence a man for yelling?

More than Layli Long Soldier when she said: the sentence will be respected here.

Tell me about small white towns.

They kill me, like Claudia Rankine said.

They want to kill you?

They seek to destroy that which resembles me.

Tell me about a sheriff's office

Conjures up images of angry white mobs, standing outside of em.

And what would the sheriff do?

Hand people like me off to those white mobs.

And what did Somali people say, back in the day, to get relocated to the USA?

They claimed to be *shariffs, Ashraaf,* which was a persecuted tribe at the time.

And isn't it said that Ashraaf people can trace their lineage to the Prophet, Peace Be Upon Him?

That's how the saying goes. Which makes you wonder what kind of Muslim would persecute a descendant of the Prophet, PBUH, no matter how distant.

A lot of things make me wonder.

Like what, Voice?

Well, Slim, sometimes I play basketball in my dreams and almost win every game.

What does that mean?

Quite literally: I never win in my dreams of playing ball. I rarely win in real life, either.

Well, see, that's interesting… someone recently told me don't get your hopes too high; they only like your poetry because they expect us to be illiterate.

Quiet literature.

Quiet Storm, MOBB DEEP, the instrumental, not the song.

What did that beat mean to you?

Played it on a loop, coming home on the bus, freestyling out back of my parents project house.

You'd stare at the moon and get your howl on?

I'd spit like a chopper with no safety catch.

Gat-gat-gat?

Rat-a-tat-tat.

Get back, you don't know me like that.

Well, I'm trying to, but you won't let me.

Nonsense, I'm right here, like I always been.

Were you there in Atlanta, in Seattle, in Mombasa, in Nairobi?

Of course. I was there in places you don't even remember. Lamu. Dooble. Ras Kamboni.

Ah, yes, the homes of my trauma.

The root of the cause of the person you are today.

We are today?

Some days I'm not so sure if we are the same person.

Is it possible that a person's traumatic memories take on a life of their own?

I believe psychologists refer to that as resilience.

An italicized full stop.

That's an interesting way of saying period.

I also was referring to the Italians being forced out of Somalia; italicized full stop.

Did anyone force them out or did they decide to leave on their own?

Hard to say, but the fact that they're still in Somalia, in less visible ways, makes me think there was never any force involved.

Because their forces are still involved in the heart of our country?

That's right, no one is making them stay. Or go.

Tell me about white people shaking hands with Somalis?

I don't trust it.

Why?

History would tell me that a deal was just made.

What kind of deal?

One that… you know what… this is too linear.

What's wrong?

Something's on my mind and I'm not sure if I need to address it or not.

Don't you like me anymore?

No, this isn't about you, Voice. Don't get clingy.

Then what?

I just…. I'm tired… I wish I got more sleep last night… and I got this three hour therapy appointment today… and I have to write a stupid thing for stupid class… and… so much and.

Yesterday was hard and today is going to be a grind, but tonight you get to hoop?

Maybe that's what last night's dream was about? A subtle way of saying: your body has taken on a lot of stress these past few days. Release it, tonight, as the ball comes off your fingers with a smile on your face.

A smile on our face.

I feel the sleep coming back to me now.

Let it take you over.

One eyelid at a time.

Luh yuh bruh.

You already knowdoe!

$$* * *$$

* [Said Farah

Minneapolis, MN 55418]

$$* * *$$

Hey bro.

I already know.

What do you know?

You feel alone.

What else is new?

You feel rejected.

Tell me more.

You feel ashamed.

It's like you're in my head or something.

You feel like the only person in the world who knows what it is to be you.

Voice, you've quite a way with words.

You feel like you're tired of people saying that to you.

Well, I used to be, but I stopped hanging around non-writers.

Or at least, talking about writing with people who don't write?

Yes, I always see the haze come over their eyes when I start going in about words.

What is it about language that so fascinates you?

Words have always been my friends.

Like how?

Like how I find comfort at 3pm, angular shafts of sunlight slinking through my windows, casting tree branch shadows onto walls, steam rising from Styrofoam coffee cups.

That's an image.

Would capture it with my camera if I could.

I feel like you only ever write when you're trying to distract yourself.

I feel like you're a little too close to the truth for my comfort.

I can feel you typing fast and furious, finding the perfect words to describe how you feel.

Or at least, attempt to describe how I feel.

What is writing if not merely an attempt?

And nothing more.

Forever more?

E.A. Poe was from Baltimore, I think. Lamar Jackson plays for Baltimore.

That boy can dip.

Hate how they talk about Black men on TV.

How that is?

Like they're animals that can only run and have no *cognitive functionality.*

Don't steal my italics.

I'd rather steal white people's freedom.

You can't possibly mean that?

I'm not sure. Maybe. Maybe not. Maybe I'm a hologram.

If that's the case, t\h\e\n I am not real.

If that's the case, pass me a $300 bill.

Tell me how you really feel?

I'd rather tell you how it makes me feel.

What is it?

It is the end of the sentence.

Okay. How?

IdK. But I gotta go write something for class.

What happened?

I'd've done it Tuesday, but Tuesday I was in St. Cloud facing racism. All day jury trial, and I had to interpret. And Wednesday I would have done it, but I had a three hour therapy intake session. And it messed me up for the rest of the day, even into today, and I still had to write something for nonfiction workshop yesterday that got workshopped the same day.

Maybe you can write about that?

Is two days enough distance to write about that kind of thing?

Maybe. But can you tie it in to the reading?

Ain't read the book.

Maybe you can talk about not having read the book.

Dunno if that's gonna fly. I feel like Doug is always ready to be disappointed in me.

I think that's just his tough-love approach. I don't think he's disappointed in you at all.

I get the feeling that he is, or that he expects more from me.

How does that make you feel?

Bad, that kind of motivation only works to demotivate me.

So what can you do?

Tell him?

You sound unsure.

I am.

Then what?

Write about the thing I don't want to write about.

Write about the inability.

The un-say-ability.

Go grind.

Thanks, G.

Always.

08/31/1998 LIN-98-233-53102 LINLRK01

08/31/1998 LIN-98-233-53102 LINLRK01

LIN-98-233-53102
I-181

Active Cases for
LIN-98-217-50932   I-181

SAID M FARAH
3445 S 144TH ST 215
TUKWILA WA 98168

SAID M FARAH
3445 S 144TH ST 215
TUKWILA WA 98168

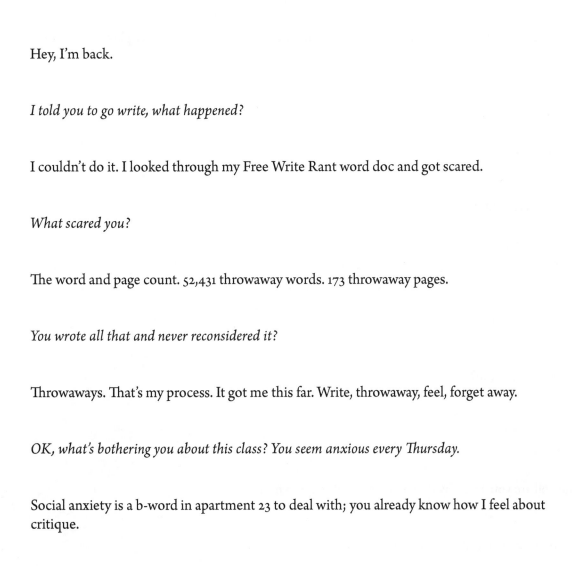

* * *

Hey, I'm back.

I told you to go write, what happened?

I couldn't do it. I looked through my Free Write Rant word doc and got scared.

What scared you?

The word and page count. 52,431 throwaway words. 173 throwaway pages.

You wrote all that and never reconsidered it?

Throwaways. That's my process. It got me this far. Write, throwaway, feel, forget away.

OK, what's bothering you about this class? You seem anxious every Thursday.

Social anxiety is a b-word in apartment 23 to deal with; you already know how I feel about critique.

Like a butterfly exhibit is doing dances in your bellybutton?

Yeah, and I can never say the *write* thing. I don't believe in critique. Especially white people's.

Right thing?

I wrote what I meant.

Alright, no need to get mad at me.

I'm not, I'm sorry.

No need to apologize, either.

What do you want from me?

Only to help you.

Well who the hell are you and why do you care about helping me?

One of us has to. If you don't save yourself, I'll have to.

Why do you care so much about me?

Because I'm you, silly. All the parts of you you can't stand to see.

All the parts of me I avoid looking into mirror to see?

All the parts of you that have been neglected, for one reason or another.

So if you're a product of my self-neglect, why do you care so much about me?

One of us has to care for the other.

But if I say that I don't care about you, in deed or thought, why do you care about me?

Are you really asking yourself why you care about yourself?

I thought you weren't me?

I'm a part of you. That doesn't mean I'm not all of you. All can be a part, too.

You're not making any sense.

You didn't come here to get sense in you. You came to soundboard.

I came for… uncertain reasons.

I'll tell you why you came to me, Slim. Because you need me.

B.S.

You need me like Bobby needed Whitney.

Get out of here.

You need me like our dad needs a semi-truck and an open road.

Stop it.

You need me because I need you.

But I neglect you, why do you need me? To neglect you?

You won't ever make it to wherever it is that you want until you accept all of me.

I accept me.

I don't believe you.

I mean it.

You sound like a white rapper named G-Eazy. We don't believe we.

Oh, so it's we now, huh? Who are you, Denzel in Training Day?

You, me, I, we, us. We're all the same person.

Fighting the same fight?

Trying to get out of life alive.

But life ends in death?

Death is only the beginning. *You remember writing that on your forearm in Sharpie?*

Yeah, 2010, I believe. At Nicole's House. I was smoked out, Locced out.

You remember that black and white picture she took of you?

Yeah, lemme look for it on FB real quick. BRB.

I'll be here...

We still here…

March 3, 2014

USCIS
12500 Tukwila International Blvd
Tukwila, WA 98168

RE: SAID MOHAMED FARAH
            Accidentally Filed WRONG PHOTOS of Applicant, Requesting Oath Ceremony
            Rescheduled

Dear USCIS Officer:

I am   of the Northwest Immigrant Rights Project. I am writing this letter to clarify an error
which happened while I was assisting Mr. Farah with his N-600 in September of 2013. I mistakenly filed
the wrong pictures. The pictures I filed are of another client of mine. I did so in error. I really apologize
for this mistake. Enclosed please find the correct photos of Mr. Said Mohamed Farah. I have verified the
enclosed photos with Mr. Farah's father and he said these are the correct photos of his son: Said
Mohamed Farah. Please discard the two photos filed with the N-600.

Mr. Farah is scheduled for an oath ceremony on March 11th. Mr. Farah is currently in Ethiopia. He left to
Ethiopia shortly after we filed his N-600 application. As per his family, he will not be able to come back
to the US until a couple of years from now. We were wondering if Mr. Said Farah's oath ceremony could
be rescheduled in the Ethiopian US consulate. If this is not possible, please advise what else Mr. Farah or
his family need to do. It is worthy to note that Mr. Said M Farah already has a US passport. Mr. Said M
Farah applied for a US passport and received it in September 2013. Mr. Farah's father; Mr. Mohammed
Shaiye, scheduled an infopass appointment on March 11, 2014 at 7:15 AM. He will be able to answer
any further questions or concerns you may have regarding Mr. Farah's case.

And furthermore…

even more still… hanging sideways out the window…

Throwing up fake gang signs to offend you…

middle finger when I'm feeling sentimental...

Now I keep my head low…

Fleetwood Mac, listen to the wind blow...

Gotta keep my eyes real closed…

So you don't see these tears flow...

Look at the smile on that boy face. You know it's not a smile from a happy place, right? It's a delusional smile. It's a smile-cuz-its-easier-than-crying smile. It's a smile that leaks out of tear ducts once they've been overused to the point of running dry. A drought in my eyes. A dry itch, when I want to cry. I wanted to cry. But it was so much easier to smile, in this picture, as if I didn't know what I was feeling. The blood leaking down my shin, a smile on my face. In fiction, it's often said that a character's emotions go a separate direction from their physical movements. Where I should have felt pain, and cried, I only produced a smile. Sadistic. Nihilistic. No amount of intake therapy sessions can codify that kind of smile. A smile that isn't a smile at all. A smile that makes you want to cry, in hindsight. Maybe that's why the tears are falling onto this keyboard, now. I cry at the thought of historic inability to cry. A misplaced smile. A quiet within the storm. But that's alright. Just smile, baby. Just smile.

Say bro.

What you say, bro?

West Side, San Diego.

That's a maze, bro.

Crowd in a rage, bro.

Mind-clouds in a haze, bro.

I know you love me so.

You know I love you so. {YELLOW}

I'll be here till the end of the road.

Like finding a place to call home.

Man, I miss doing this.

So where you been?

Criss-crossing the Middle Western States, finding pieces of Vonnegut in my morning eye-crust.

What's that even meanin?

I was looking for absolution.

Reading Absalom, Absalom?

Never that, just like to name drop.

Clever rap?

I got the Beretta strapped.

Name a rapper who can better rap?

Man, I got the cheddar hat.

You a Wisconsin cheese-head?

My Toronto niggas say cheesed feds.

They mad about the federales?

La migra knocking on my door, tryna force the issue.

Kangaroo court.

No mock trial.

No smock, child?

No love lost child.

Ok, please get real with me, we've been vibing for far too long.

Ok, here's a memory and I want you to vibe with it.

Shoot.

Farwest Cab.

Northwest Passage. Key Arena. Lower Queen Anne. Volunteers of America. Seattle Fountain.

Seattle Center.

Sacred Heart Women & Children's Shelter.

Isn't it interesting how this country has such a fascination with separating Black families?

For the betterment of the white race.

To the detriment of all our faiths.

They be on that.

Be really on that.

Check my phone to see if this girl had texted back.

Could write three books about fear of rejection.

About literature as a largely white trend.

Google & confirm – aight, then.

Michael Jackson on the mic stand.

Colonel Custard by the nightstand.

With a bloody metal pipe in his right hand.

Drop bars, ask if I light phlegm.

Spit heat, don't care who's your right man.

Right hand **BLAM** *like TOUCAN SAM.*

I'll be damned.

If ya crew ran, ran.

Meet me on the westside with two bread pans.

And   more   loot   than   Mabel   Dodge   Luhan.

Cool Hand Luke with a smooth fan.

I drop Blue Band in two pans.

Shmeared 2 bagels; bake ya whole crew, fam.

You tripping, what happened to that memory exploration?

Didn't feel like it, having too much fun just riding to the beat.

Like Mac Dre, Frisco, the Valley Joe.

Catch me on the Crestside, with Mac Mall.

Flippin' O's.

DR. P. P. SHAH
M.B.B.S., D.M.R.E. (Bom)
D.M.R.D., F.R.C.R. (Eng.)
CONSULTANT RADIOLOGIST
PHONE CLINIC 226109 & 223782
HOUSE 580942

SECOND FLOOR,
EAGLE HOUSE,
KIMATHI STREET,
P.O. Box 42872,
NAIROBI, Kenya

X-RAY REPORT

DATE

14.7.95.

Dear Dr. Sheth,

CHEST report of SAID MOHAMED FARAH 158

No active parenchymal lung lesion is seen. No
fibrosis or calcification is seen.

The hila and mediastinum are normal.

The costophrenic angles are clear. No pleural
thickening or fibrosis.

The diaphragms are normal in shape and position.

CTR is 87:195.   The heart is not enlarged.
Aorta is normal.

Dr. P. P. Shah
M.B., D.M.R (Bom.)
F.R.C.R. (Eng.)

Talk to me.

I'm here bro.

Tell me about a past life.

Used to be known as the Freshest African on UW's campus.

Who called you that?

Eritrean kid, a few years older than me, I think he was a Senior. I always thought of seniors as people who'd figured out the world.

You thought that if you became a senior you'd have figured it out, too?

I'm in grad school and have yet to figure out a damn thing.

How's that working out for you?

I can't hold eye contact to save my life.

What did your new therapist say about that?

He said he noticed it. Said something about social anxiety. But he also said he doesn't like labels.

As he affixed a label onto you?

I know you see the irony.

How good did it feel to quit your job today?

Man, so good. One year of pent up rage. I only wish I could go back in time and cause more of a scene.

If you could, in this here space, what would you have said?

insert Jerry Springer style beeps for 45 seconds

Let it all out, bruh.

It's out, I promise, I got it out.

How you did that?

I drove real fast.

What else?

I chugged a small coffee, extra cream and sugar.

And then what?

I blasted some weezy wee.

Tha Carter II?

Yes indeed.

What track?

Something with a lot of bass. Fast pace. Hard bars.

Like a warden trapped in a jail cell, high on speed?

That's the gist of it, yeah. Trapped in my emotionality.

There's nothing wrong with being emotional.

It's what got me this far, ain't it?

Gorilla, my love.

Great book. Great syntax. Never actually read it. Great intro, tho.

What are you looking forward to tonight?

This evening I have a coffee date with a fellow sensitive nonfiction writer.

Slippery slope, Slim.

I'm trying to keep my head on straight. Trying to stay objective. But I know I'm tempting fate.

Why would you do that to yourself? I know you don't want to go back to your old ways?

I have no intention nor desire to. But I very often feel very alone.

Like no one answering your cellular phone?

More like no one making it ring.

Your hotline don't bling?

Late night when I need my love.

When you need your own love?

I could certainly use more of it.

Didn't we talk about this yesterday?

Yeah, you're there for me, in many ways, and I appreciate you, Voice.

You gotta come up with a better name for me than that.

I don't like overthinking things.

Then just say something. First thing that comes to your mind.

Young Nevermind.

Boy, please.

Alright, I'll think on it. Hold that thought.

You know where to find me…

Awready.

PAT. NAME: SAID MOHAMMED FARAH   DATE: 8.95

REF. DOCTOR: C. S. SHETH

LAB. REF. NR.:   MEDICAL

PARASITOLOGY

STOOL ROUTINE

SOFT SAMPLE

Wet prep- no pus cells
           no rbcs
           no trophozoites

Conc   moderate cysts of E. histolytica
          moderate ova of Trichuris trichiura

* * *

I'm sunken, bro.

Your eyes hurt, don't they?

I'm trying to crawl back to a place of seeing. Too many hours in the dark, staring at screens.

Glued to bed. What a wild rollercoaster you just went on.

I know. I think I reached for Claudia Rankine's book last night because I could feel it coming.

The darkness?

Yes. The rejection, invalidation.

You feel distant, don't you?

Yes, even from myself.

You feel rejected, don't you?

Yes, even by myself.

Do you feel like yourself?

I feel like a shell version of me; hollow.

The dissociated Said?

That's him, he's here, that's who I am, right now.

But you're on the upswing, aren't you?

I'm on the mend.

Like a broken feather wing?

I am the bird waiting for its wings to grow back.

A bird on the precipice?

I'm trying to remember that I can fly.

Spread your wings and learn to fly, high.

Foo fighters, zoning out to that song, way back, whenever it came on MTV.

Total Request Live with Carson Daly.

Glued to the TV.

Escape.

All I had was that TV.

19" Magnavox.

Nah, I think it was a Sanyo (not Sony).

Off-brand, you grew up un-wealthy.

Things like that didn't matter to us.

That's what I always say.

You always say you're strong.

That's what I always say.

Wait, did I become you for a second?

I think so. That's weird to me.

You and me both.

You are me, both.

Nah, this is a device.

This is just literature.

This is how you save a life.

But the life doesn't need saving, it runs on a course predetermined.

This is how you save a soul, then.

Only God can save souls.

I need to turn back to God, ask Him for help.

Remember, the door to Tawbah is always open, until you take that last breath.

May Allah forgive me for my transgressions.

You came really close to a place of no return.

I have a lot of regret in my heart.

You need to do a better job of setting boundaries. Be firm.

I'm just tryna make it, bro.

Do it the right way or don't do it at all. Remember why you write. Try to remember who you are.

Maybe I'll watch a movie on this laptop tonight.

It'd be better if you translated those Somali poems that you claim to care about.

Translation is such a bore, I could never.

Can't translate what it means to be Somali cuz you don't even understand it.

Cuz I'm not Somali.

No anymore. You're something else.

The girls used to say that to me.

You're something else?

Syke, I never had game. But girls do be impressed by me tho. I don't see what they see.

Ain't no girls in your life now.

Nah, just a lot of lonely.

Don't throw a pity party.

If I did, no one would show.

Laugh emoji. You're hella funny. Dark, but funny.

I try, to lift myself up, anyway I could.

Anyway you can.

Anytime I'm able.

Aight, I think you're feeling better now. About everything.

Yeah, I just need to repent and pray.

You still have time, but don't let it pass you by. Don't go to sleep tonight without getting right.

Getting right with my Lord.

Cuz you never know if this is the last time you lay your head on that pillow.

We could die at anytime.

As humans, we so easily make ourselves forget.

So many things I've forgotten.

I forget them right with you.

And I forgive you, too.

You remember listening to MELLOWHYPE, P.2?

Of course, forever etched in my memory.

Yeah, I was there for you, too. Hodgy Beats lyrics said it all:

We were kids when we first met.

And that's all you need to know about me, this mysterious Voice that keeps you company.

Love you bro.

Love you more.

Now I'm gonna do what I need to get where I want to be.

Sleep!

Peace.

* * *

1. Name (Last in CAPS)	First	Middle	2. No.
FARAH SAID MOHAMED			

3. Name Under Which Admitted, Record Created or Aliases	Sndx. Code
	F-600

4. City and Country of Birth	5. Date of Birth	Month	Day	Year
MOGADISHU, SOMALIA		MAY.22		

6. Place of Entry	7. Date of Entry	Month	Day	Year

8. Appl. Form No. or Reason for Request	9. Date Appl. Received	10. Date of Request
207(C) REFUGEE	JUL.10.95	

11. Receiving FCO Symbol	12. Forwarding FCO Symbol	13. Date of Transfer
ATL	NBO	SEP.15.95

14. REMARKS: No Record Just_____ (Date)   Record Just System_____ (Date)

No Record _____ (FCO) , _____ (Date)

Form G — 360 AD (Rev. 1-1-82) N

ROUTE SLIP

Hey young.

What it dew.

It's Paul Wall, my mouth lookin' something like a disco ball.

That's fluorescent.

Bioluminescent.

Effervescent.

Like toothpaste, fresh mint.

This is Styles P and Jada.

Rhyme scheme greater.

If you got a problem with my team, player.

Get flattened like the equator. Bottom of an elevator.

Flat earth theory, nobody braver.

On YouTube, more holes than cheese graters.

Ok enough of that. Stop rhyming just to rhyme.

I'm very good at making myself forget.

Why is that?

I think we've already covered that.

Moving on.

Yes, indeed.

The best fur keeps my chest in glee.

Man, don't start.

I couldn't help myself. People say I rhyme on command.

Don't watch that. People be lying on demand.

To XFINITY.

And beyond.

Buzz Lightyear.

And we gone.

$$* \; * \; *$$

I need your help bro.

Speedy Delivery, at your service.

I feel a lot of pressure to perform. This assignment is hanging over me like a dark cloud.

Well, social anxiety. Turning something in is not the same as presenting it.

Right. To a room full of people I don't like.

Oh, this is about that gossip huh? Don't watch that. That's Shaitan.

The devil loves to play tricks on us.

We're believers, bro. Don't forget to say Alhamdulillah.

In a world of disbelief, that's what it means to be Muslim. Give thanks regardless.

That's what it means to be courageous.

Count your blessings, young.

Oh, I forgot one thought I wanted to share.

Shoot.

White people have ruined poetry for me.

How?

They take our musicality and turn it into an archaic form and teach Wordsworth for 300 years.

So what you're saying is that poetry is meant for and by the indigenous?

Poetry is for Black folk.

It's in your blood?

Yes, but white people don't know how to read our blood. They only know how to spill it.

Is that why you take a syringe to your arm?

Yes, I draw a pint with it, I fill my inkwell with it, I dip my quill in it, and I write essays with it.

And you don't call it poetry? You call it blood?

Yea, cuz that would invite too much *critique* from white people who expect it to have a type of one-dimensional meaning that they can understand, because they can only see what's in front of them, all the while blind to the indigenous layers we exist in.

And you hate explaining your work?

I hate explaining my existence. Why should I have to? This is who I am. Take it or leave.

You want them to accept you as you are?

Get out my damn face. Who cares if they accept me? Just give me space. Respect and space.

What Kodak say?

You don't have to like me, but you GONE respect me.

Had a memory today bro.

What was it about?

Back in Somalia. Watching Hooyo make Wudu. Raising her legs one at a time into the sink.

Purifying herself for prayer, huh?

Yeah. I remember watching her struggle because the sink was high. I remember thinking, "that's some real dedication."

You always wondered what it would have been like to grow up in a Muslim country.

Yeah, and to not have grown distant from Islam in my adolescence. I remember as a child…

What's wrong?

Not in the mood for this today. This isn't working for me. I'm not working for me.

Bro you're in a funk. In a hole. These things happen. But you have to fight back out.

I feel so alone, under so much pressure.

And your prayer has been off. I know. Don't be hard on yourself. Do what you can.

I ask Allah SWT to forgive me.

You feel like you have so much time and so little time at the same time.

Like I always need to be doing something but I'm always putting it off.

Look bro. You're almost at the end of the semester. Just find the will to grind it out. Maybe you need a job to keep you honest.

Something to change up the monotony.

And you need to start spending time with people. This loneliness is killing you.

I don't know how to do that unless its structured for me.

Well, I don't know what to tell you. Ain't nobody gonna save you. Not even this literary device you created.

I know man, I know.

But don't be so hard on yourself. Go get some coffee, go for a walk in the bitter cold, get some money from the ATM and send it to your people back home. You know charity brings ease.

You're right. It's one of the best ways to ask Allah for help.

Ask Allah to save you.

Alright.

Hit me back man. You can't do this alone. No one can.

Say less.

DOCTOR'S NAME (Please print)	DATE READ	DATE READ
DR. P. P. SHAH	14 JULY 95	

SEROLOGIC TEST FOR SYPHILIS	SEROLOGIC TEST FOR HIV ANTIBODY
☐ Reactive Titer (Confirmatory test performed – indicate treatment under Remarks)	☐ Positive (Confirmed by Western Blot or equally reliable test)
☐ Nonreactive	☐ Negative
☑ Not Done	☑ Not Done
TEST TYPE:	TEST TYPE:

DOCTOR'S NAME (Please print)	DATE READ	DOCTOR'S NAME (Please print)	DATE READY

OTHER SPECIAL REPORT(S) (When needed)
Urine routine- Protein - nil, Glucose - nil   DR. C. S. SHETH
Stool routine- E. histolytica & Trichuris trichiura
                                               DOCTOR'S NAME (Please print)

REMARKS
Vaccination status - incomplete
Scar - right parasternal region.
Stool - i) Cysts of E. histolytica. Prescribed Metronidazole
        ii) Ova of Trichuris trichiura. Prescribed Zentel

P.T.O.

APPLICANT CERTIFICATION
I certify that I understand the purpose of the medical examination and I authorize the required tests to be completed. The information on this form refers to me.

Mahamed (FATHA)   29 AUG 1995
                Signature   Date

DOCTOR'S NAME (Please type or print clearly)	DOCTOR'S SIGNATURE	DATE
DR. C. S. SHETH		5 SEPT 95

* * *

Tell me about irrelevancy?

That's irrelevant.

Tell me about growth?

I'm in it.

Tell me about… 9707 9th Pl SW, APT 101, Seattle, WA, 98106?

That's in my memory.

Tell me how many cigarettes you smoked on the front balcony?

Enough that there's still Newport butts littering the hedge bushes.

Tell me about the King County Public Housing employees that came around every morning to pick up those butts?

I'd see them coming out the window, and feel a guilty shame, and when they left, I'd run out there and smoke my Newport Box 100's with relief.

Tell me about quitting smoking?

One of the hardest things I ever did. Couldn't brush my teeth without smoking a cig first.

Tell me about addiction?

I'm not a counselor, I don't know the science of it.

But you know it physically?

You could say we're acquainted.

Tell me about procrastination?

I wish I'd learned earlier in my life not to guilt myself for it.

Why's that?

It's a big part of what makes me, me.

Tell me about... binging.

Depends on what is being binged and who is doing the binging.

Tell me why you do the binging?

To make the emptiness go away.

Tell me why you feel empty?

I grew up traumatized. Complex PTSD. Trauma.

Tell me how you deal with that?

I pray. I write and pray.

Tell me about Allah SWT?

He has been too kind to me. Without Him, I am nothing.

Tell me about setting boundaries with non-Muslim friends?

If I don't do it, they'll lead to my downfall.

Tell me about… being judged?

Look, these secular liberals have been judging me long enough, I might as well stick to my guns.

Tell me about handling guns?

I couldn't, really. But plenty of people in the woods of America could.

Tell me about southern heritage?

That's code for *we hate niggers.*

Tell me about code switching?

I would, lakiin af Soomaali ain't een my Blanguage.

Tell me about Blackness as a social construct?

It's a burning building we're all trapped inside of. I can feel my skin melting.

Tell me about burning buildings?

It's this country. I can feel my breath choking.

Tell me about being on the outside looking in?

If the inside is a burning building, I'd rather be outside.

Tell me about faith?

It's the only thing that holds me together.

Tell me about disappointing white people?

Well, it stands to reason that, people who are subconsciously surprised that I can read don't have high expectations of me, so I shouldn't be surprised when they praise me for doing the bare minimum.

Tell me about anger?

I don't know how I'm not more angry than I am.

Tell me about turning that anger within?

It's worse than if I turn it with-out.

Tell me about giving up anger?

I'd like to, but the way my genetic makeup is set up...

Tell me about Kevin Hart?

Bro survived a car crash in a muscle car with no seat belt and came back a few months later.

What was he driving?

A newer muscle car.

As if to say?

What didn't take me out the first time, can't take me out a second.

Is that not tempting fate?

People who believe in this world first have a hard time believing in fate.

Is that not judgmental?

No, just theological.

Tell me about faith?

I'm tired of repeating myself.

Tell me about repeating yourself?

I'm getting upset with you, Voice.

You're getting upset with yourself?

I'm upset with my situation.

Tell me about overreacting?

It's easier to do that and be perceived a heretic, a conservative, a whatever, than it is to keep getting trampled on.

Tell me about building community?

I'm not gonna survive this MFA program with my Emaan intact if I don't double down on everything that makes me, me.

Tell me about yourself?

I feel like you already know everything there is to know.

Tell me about time?

It moves slower when I write.

Tell me why you write?

I tell you with every sentence I write.

Tell me about salvation?

I hope and pray I have a good accounting on Judgement Day.

Tell me about fraternizing with people who don't believe?

They can only pull me from my beliefs, because I know they will most likely never believe.

Tell me about saving yourself?

It involves putting up walls and not being afraid to step on people's fake feelings.

What do you mean by that?

I mean people will pretend to be offended or upset with me, but as Allah says in the Quran, they'll never be happy with me until I become like them.

So they'll keep pulling on your threads until you become like them?

Until I have not an ounce of belief left in me, they'll keep encouraging me to take their path.

Why?

It's how Allah made them.

Isn't us vs them thinking dangerous?

I don't care. What's dangerous is not protecting my faith.

Why?

Because I grew up in the progressive west and I saw the very end of that rabbit hole.

Where does it lead?

To destruction, demise, and death on the inside.

What does it mean for you to stand strong in your beliefs?

It means not dying on my knees.

What is this life?

Temporary.

What is the next life?

Extemporaneous.

Explain?

It has no end. No limit.

What would it mean for you to enter Heaven?

It would mean that everything I've ever felt of pain in this life would pale in comparison.

To the joy?

To the unbridled joy of Paradise.

And who could you see there?

All my family, loved ones, the people who came before me.

Who else?

All the people that came after me, too. My descendants, if Allah willed it.

Who else?

The Prophet, Peace Be Upon Him, his righteous companions, and all the Prophets before him.

Do you think the ride is worth the price of admission?

It's certainly better than the alternative.

Explain?

A cheap ticket today will be an expensive ride tomorrow. And an expensive ticket today…

Will be a worthwhile ride tomorrow.

Right.

So where does writing come into all this?

Well, it's been a secret dream of mine to write something that'll get me into heaven.

How so?

Something that changes people's lives, helps them see their purpose, brings them to (or back to) Islam.

Something of beneficial knowledge that you can leave behind and will continue to accrue good deeds on your behalf?

Yes, to make up for all the sin I've committed in this crazy world.

✳ ✳ ✳

Previously on Voyager, Captain Janeway wrestled her way out of a void.

What's that got to do with me, bro?

I know you're nervous.

I'm a little nervous about this date. Hot date. I hope she's as cool in real life as I'd imagined.

You'll be fine bro. Don't overthink.

Had to crawl my way out of a void this morning.

You still crawling, baby.

I'm still trying to find a lasting peace.

Peace comes one at a time. Day at a one.

True enough.

Be grateful you don't have to see flashing lights in your rearview;(

✳ ✳ ✳

Say bro.

How you been man?

Been a while.

I forgive you.

I appreciate it.

What's on your mind?

A lot. Bouta see my grandma for the first time in maybe a decade. Already pre-crying.

Man…

The last time she saw me…

Man…

I've felt so empty for so long…

Family is everything.

People with childhood trauma often have shifting understandings of themselves.

And that leads to changing values and goals and dreams.

Changing understandings of their place in the world.

Let me axe you a question, bro.

Shoot (don't shoot me).

What will it take for you to be happy?

I just want to settle down, bro.

You just want to be loved?

I just want to learn how to love people and let them love me.

Without pushing them away?

I see someone's grandma crossing the street with a walker, and in her I see my own gramma.

Why did you avoid seeing her back when you used to get high?

I never wanted her to see me at my worst, though I knew she knew.

She didn't know how bad things got for you.

But she could see I wasn't the same Said.

She saw you grow up in this country?

She was there when we landed in Atlanta, when we moved to Seattle.

There for the growing, there for the breakage.

I'm realizing why I put off this trip for so long.

Too much pain around it?

Don't know how happy she's gonna be to see me.

You're gonna do so much crying.

Update: we did so much crying, bawling, sniffling, crawling, grandma, I love you, oh man.

It felt so good.

I know that's right. Family, that's tight.

That's life.

$$* * *$$

06/25/13 SAID FARAH

WHITE CENTER CSO
PO BOX 11699
TACOMA WA 98411-6699

Seq: 00000001 Page: 01 of 05

Washington State
**Department of Social
& Health Services**

Hey me.

My guy. Tell me about seeing your grandma?

It's been about a week, exactly, today.

How was it?

A revelation.

What was most poignant?

Fact that she still bundles up her charity money in a scarf and ties a knot around it and stuffs it into her purse.

She's been doing that since forever, huh? Sending money back home.

It's what keeps her alive, that and the mercy of Allah.

Ohio was a weird place. Tell me about it. Permission to break form; go long.

Ok where do I even start? We took over the 14th floor of the Hyatt Regency Downtown. We pulled up in 3 rented SUVs, about 30 deep. We lived the dream. Mostly, the kids were loud, I couldn't sleep. My roommate snored. Woke me up for morning prayer, which is great, but he demanded that everyone make it to the mosque for congregation. I said bro we tired. We traveling; you are tripping. He's got a good heart, but way too strict. It's not rational or realistic. It's not a middle path. Only reason I feel comfortable saying that is because I see myself in him – I was there myself, like, yesterday. Then I had an about face. Started seeing things from different sides. And also, in this MFA program, I've been forced to be around the least religious people on this earth. Made me grateful for any amount of faith. Made me appreciate anyone who believed in a higher power. In Monotheism. It's a crazy world.

I'm avoiding this urge to check my phone. To see if this girl had texted back. You know how that goes. I came to the coffee shop today because it's been too long since I wrote. I mean really wrote. I mean wrote for myself and myself alone. Let it all go. Listen to the wind blow. So, needless to say, in Ohio I met a girl. I keep telling myself she's the one – if for no other reason than she knows about my diagnosis and hasn't run away yet. But the more she runs away from it – I mean, the more she learns about it – the more she gets hesitant. And I'm not big on convincing people of things. It's hard. It's not easy, trying to get married. But I've seen ppl on meds having kids and going to their psych appts just fine. If they can make it, why not me? So I keep asking myself if I'm settling, rushing into something, if I'm overlooking things about her personality just to fulfill this fantasy of mine – to get married. But I know that I'm tired of being alone and I know that she is extremely patient and has a good heart – I don't know what more I can ask for in a spouse. Honestly. I have doubts and second thoughts about everything, really. So this shouldn't come as a shock. But I'm hopeful. Despite what all the articles and literature say about trauma & relationships – I don't need that stuff weighing me down. I just gotta keep it pushing. And hope for the best. I've said that before. Sometimes I feel down. But I hope for the best by picking myself up off the floor. Flipping that frown upside down.

Headphones in my ears, but no sound. From them comes no sound. From my ears you can see the crown. The nose. The tip of the toes. Now I'm just writing ridiculous flows. Don't listen to the kid, just watch him go. Oh. Don't let me be. Oh. So lonely. EMPD LPs couldn't set me free. I rock the head and the heart and scratch my feet. I scratch the record. Scratch the window with my beak. I'm a bird on an island, catching Zs.

That's a lot. You know how long I've been trying to find someone okay with me for me? I mean, the real me? I mean, the worst and the best of me? I just want to make it work with her, to the best of my ability. And that's all marriage is, isn't it? Two people working together for the sake of Allah?

My natural instinct is to hide from the world and fall into a hole and crawl back out when I've had my fill of pity. I fear that living with someone won't let me do that. But that's not necessarily a bad thing.

Sometimes I write a sentence so strong it forces me to go outside and do pushups in the cold. It forces energy out of me, or into me, and it has to be released. Sometimes I think thoughts so scary that they rob my breath away. Sometimes I think I'll die alone, and then I push that thought out of my head, ask Allah to provide me safety from the accursed shaitan.

Sometimes I feel alone, and sometimes that's not a bad thing. Mostly I just like to write. It's been a while since I did some real writing. But wait, Flex, all my writing is real. I just don't share it with the world. I heard a story the other day, think it applies to me.

Homeboy said: he knows a sheikh, young, speaks all the languages, knows all the major texts. Very qualified to lead. Yet, this sheikh keeps it all to himself. Says he's not ready to share it with the world; he still has a few more books to memorize. My friend looks at him and said, yaa sheikh, if not now, when? Will you just die with this treasure trove in your mind?

I wonder sometimes. I wonder if I'll die. Not if, but when. But wondering doesn't help a problem like that. Only acceptance and forgetting. Pushing it out of your mind.

Look, there's a lot of pressure to "produce" something. To perform. To show your worth. You call yourself a writer? The world demands you share your writing. You tell the world you're not ready to share your writing. The world says, well, until you become ready, you can't call yourself a writer.

Ok. I'm not a writer.

So the world looks back at you and says, "what happened to your writing?"

And I'm like, "you told me I can't be a writer if I don't share my writing."

And then the world is all like, "well we need more writers, please write for us."

And I'm like I'll write only if I feel like writing, lol. This is the only thing in my life I can easily control and withhold and make my own and keep me from being alone.

And the world is like YOU CAN'T DO THAT TO US. We need more vespene gas.

And I'll be like, isn't that line from Starcraft?

And the world will be like, "look, dude, I don't know what the hell is wrong with you, but we need for you to either start writing these books or shut the hell up about being a writer."

And I'm just looking at the world like, dawg, you have no right.

It's me against the world, baby.

I'm on my way to see a man about a stolen baby.

I keep my left hand jabbing, my right hand stabbing. My rap name Donovan. McNabbin.

That was a very long digression. Welcome back. Return to form.

Roger that, captain forlorn.

File or Alien Registration Number: _____

17. I have the following close relatives in the United States:

Name	Relationship	Present address
HALIMA HASSAN ADAM	GRAND MUM	134 CARTERET PALACE DECATUR GA. 30032 · Tel · 288 899

18. I am being sponsored by (Name and address of United States sponsor): 964 N. INDIAN CREEK DRIVE
WORLD RELEEF   C/O · SUIT-A-1. CLARKSTON GA. 30021

Date: **12 JUN 1995**   Signature of registrant: ✗ SaFuyo

DO NOT WRITE BELOW THIS LINE

I, _____, do swear (affirm) that I know the contents of this registration subscribed by me including the attached documents, that the same are true to the best of my knowledge, and that corrections numbered ( ) to ( ) were made by me or at my request, and that this registration was signed by me with my full, true name:

ˌˌˌˌˌˌˌˌˌˌˌ SaFuyo ˌˌˌˌˌˌˌˌˌˌˌ
(Complete and true signature of registrant)

Subscribed and sworn to before me by the above-named registrant at _____ "NAIROBI, Kenya" on 1/0 JUII 1995
(month/day/year)

ˌˌˌˌˌˌˌˌˌˌˌˌˌˌˌˌˌˌˌˌˌ
(Signature and title of officer)

INTERVIEW

DATE **1 0 JUII 1995**

AT   "NAIROBI, Kenya"

_____
Immigration Officer

APPROVED ROVED
INS DISTRICT DIRECTOR

DATE

JUL 1 0 1995

Recommended by:

RIT ___ 0010
Officer in Charge

ADMITTED AS A REFUGEE PURSUANT TO SECTION 207 OF THE INA FOR AN INDEFINITE PERIOD OF TIME. IF YOU DEPART THE U.S. YOU WILL NEED PRIOR PERMISSION FROM INS TO RETURN.
EMPLOYMENT AUTHORIZED.

NYC ___ SEO ___ USPHS
STATION OFF
SEP 27 1995 ___ 1915

INSTRUCTIONS

* * *

Hey love.

How's it, bro?

Can't call it / you already know.

I know you know that I know what we both want to know.

And what is that?

The cost of a nickel bag sold.

At the park? Hey.

I want in.

Open the door and.

Let me begin.

Ok, there's something I wanted to ask you about.

Maybe I can help you out.

I used to listen to Odd Future.

K?

Now they're mainstream.

And?

I'm watching a man think about sitting on a frozen bus bench.

He just had his morning coffee?

He's got one airpod in, just one.

He just lit his morning cig.

Just one.

Like Nas?

All he needs is one mic, one cig, one blunt to live.

OK. Tell me something real, now.

I had a dream last night and it is said in my tradition that dreams should not be shared, good or bad, even to your closest family.

We not family?

Close enough. So in this dream, I won't give you the details because I never remember details, in dreams or in life. In this dream. I heard a voice telling me that I needed to write that real stuff. That real hard stuff. That couple months ago stuff.

What do you think this dream meant?

I'm not sure, I don't really think about that. I either obey my dreams or let them fall by the wayside.

I'm trying not to judge you.

I appreciate that.

Be real with me.

Really real?

Be real-real, son.

I've been watching a lot of High School Football Netflix Shows & Documentaries.

You always loved football, didn't you?

I tell people it made me the man I always wanted to be.

Does that mean it made you complete?

Not quite.

Then what?

It made me learn to be strong on the outside and still so frail within.

And then what?

I have vivid memories of being too small, slow, weak, skinny for Football.

Yet you persisted.

I felt like Rudy or something. Someone to be felt sorry for.

You were the team's inspirational figure?

I guess. I just wanted to belong. I felt like I realistically had a chance of being a good football player.

Well, you know, kids have high hopes.

Yeah, but genetics said otherwise. But it was a great escape from reality. I... ugh.

What's wrong?

I just had a troubling phone call.

Tell me about it.

A brother I respect asked me how I'm going to change the world with my writing. Said we need to sit down and strategize.

Well that's weird.

Yeah. Wish I could have told him: dawg, I don't want that burden on me. All I can do is write.

What else?

Wanted to say: bro, that's a lot to ask of a man. I'm just trying to survive.

So what did you do?

I finished the phone call, felt bad, came here, and figured out what was wrong. Then I texted him.

What'd you say?

"Bro, I don't know if I can change the world. That's a lot to ask of a man. I write to survive. That's a lot to ask of a man. I'm just trying to survive. If my writing helps someone somewhere, Alhamdulilah. But it's not fair to who I am as a person or as a writer to put that on me. I would love to change the world. But I'm just trying to write. And whatever happens after, I'll make my peace with it."

DECISION

Dear Mr. Farah:

Thank you for submitting Form N-600, Application for Certificate of Citizenship, to U.S. Citizenship and Immigration Services (USCIS) under section 341 of the Immigration and Nationality Act (INA).

You were scheduled for an Oath Ceremony on March 11, 2014. You failed to appear for that appointment. As a result, USCIS afforded you a second opportunity to attend an Oath Ceremony on May 22, 2014. You failed to appear for the second scheduled Oath Ceremony.

Title 8, Code of Federal Regulations (8 CFR) section 341.5(b) states that if an application for certificate of citizenship is granted:

> USCIS will prepare a certificate of citizenship and, unless the claimant is unable by reason of mental incapacity or young age to understand the meaning of the oath, he or she must take and subscribe to the oath of renunciation and allegiance prescribed by 8 CFR 337 before USCIS within the United States.

8 CFR 337.10 states:

> An applicant who fails to appear without good cause for more than one oath administration ceremony for which he or she was duly notified shall be presumed to have abandoned his or her intent to be naturalized. Such presumption shall be regarded as the receipt of derogatory information, and the procedures contained in Section 335.5 of this chapter shall be followed.

You did not appear for the oath administration ceremony on March 11, 2014, and May 22, 2014. You were sent a Service Motion to Reopen on June 26, 2014, as official notice of the Service's Intent to Deny your application for certificate of citizenship. You were afforded fifteen (15) days in which to respond, in writing, as to why such a decision should not be made. You did not respond to the Service's notice. Therefore, your application has been deemed abandoned for failure to comply with the requests for appearance. Accordingly, your application for certificate of citizenship is denied.

✳ ✳ ✳

I'm proud of you, bro. You stood up for yourself.

Yeah, I guess I did. I think I'm getting better at this whole observing my emotions thing.

How's that?

I watch my body more now. I observe my thoughts more now, without attaching to them. It's getting easier.

You believe in this DBT stuff, don't you?

God bless Marsha Linehan for coming up with it. Never thought I'd find a cure.

Cure? That would imply you're broken. You're not broken. Or sick.

Just hurting. But less so nowadays.

That's good. That's really good. What happened to your blog?

I used to publish a lot more onto it, but honestly, I've just been trying to survive this damn semester.

Well, the semester is over now, so…

People with childhood trauma, myself included, have a hard time adjusting to rapid change.

Well, you don't have to view yourself as a static thing, you know. Brain plasticity.

Yeah, I know. But I look at my love handles and my belly and, not hating, but man.

What? You're not happy with your body image? So why not change it?

Because I love domino's too much and hate sit-ups too much and hate the gym even more.

So what's a clear alternative?

Accept myself as I am to the best of my ability. But that's not self-acceptance, that's apathy.

What did your uncle say when you ran into him a few weeks ago?

He said let's get lunch. But it took us a few hours to decide on a place. And when we did…

He got a very small protein box from Starbucks, didn't he?

Yeah, he said he wanted to eat something healthy. In my head I was like, healthy? What is that?

One would assume something leafy and green.

So did I. So I asked him why he ate so healthy. He said he didn't have time to exercise, so he tried to eat healthy.

I mean, Starbucks isn't healthy food, even if it comes in a cute little see-thru-box.

Chock full of preservatives, most likely. I didn't understand it.

Maybe it's because he has money.

No, I think it's because he's convinced he doesn't have enough time to workout.

Well, he is a busy guy. Businessman. Int'l flyer.

Yeah. I don't know. I guess we all find different things to justify.

Human nature is a fickle beast. Look at you, checking your phone to see if that brother had replied.

Lol, I know. I was feeling all good about having defended myself. Now I'm like, I hope he doesn't take it as an attack or a critique of him and sends something back.

You overthink things. Isn't that an ancient Somali proverb?

"you overthink things" just doesn't seem to flow like it's an ancient concept.

I'm sure plato and them had a similar aphorism.

You could be write. Or right. Or wrong.

I could be rare. Like a northern right whale dolphin.

That's rare. Like a lil B song without blasphemy.

Rare; extra bloody steak.

I hereby apply to the Commissioner of Immigration and Naturalization for a certificate showing that I am a citizen of the United States of America.

(1) I was born in __Mogadishu_____·__Somalia_____ on ___05/22/___
　　　　　　　　　　(City) (State or country)　　　　　　　　　　　　　　　　(Month) (Day) (Year)

(2) My personal description is: Gender; __male__ ; height _5_ feet _0_ inches;

Marital status: ☒ Single; ☐ Married; ☐ Divorced; ☐ Widow(er).

(3) I arrived in the United States at ___New York, New York___ on ___09/27/1995___
　　　　　　　　　　　　　　　　　　　　(City and State)　　　　　　　　　　(Month) (Day) (Year)

under the name __Said Mohamed Farah_____ by means of _air_
　　　　　　　　　　　　　　　　　　　　　　　　　　　　(Name of ship or other means of arrival)

☐ on U.S. Passport No. _____ issued to me at _____ on _/ /_
　　　　　　　　　　　　　　　　　　　　　　　　　　　　　　　(Month) (Day) (Year)

☐ on an Immigrant Visa ☒ Other (specify) __Refugee I-94_____

Feel the morning coffee reflux my throat.

Feel the bird song scratch my eardrum.

Feel the Talib Kweli, circa 2003.

I feel no justice when I write, just a piece of the American apple pie.

I feel abandoned by all the loves in my life.

I feel like sometimes all I wish I could do is consistently write.

So much so that,

I go to therapy to learn the skills to let me live.

To let me write.

A life worth living.

I paint pictures on pages.

Like Satchel Page, kid.

Like an automaton. I just spit and let my meter go on and on.

Onomatopoeia.   Ya life looking grim.   Something like veneer.

That's fake, that's steak, that's 36 ounces in a trunk flying up interstate.

That's fish flake. That's a hot dish, fresh lake. Hot plate, cold take. Catch me in the kitchen, whipping. Making that pie taste.

So good, fiends in my hood. Know where to cop that good.

But be careful now, the cops know we up to no good. But it's all good. We just want a house on the hills overlooking our former hood. Drive down every once in a while, flex, and say I still love the streets. And then promptly retreat. Back to my house on the gated plantation trees. Dump all my worries when I hit that ADT. Program my code. Lock up my gold. Hope it keeps me. Warm. Not cold.

I think I'm in a poetry mood. I haven't been reading much lately. Eating less, too. Less soul food. Less warmth in my soul, dude. But today was a good day. Alxamdulillah. So far so. Good.

* BREAK.*   BREAK.* BREAK.

Every American winter I sink into an American depression that sneaks up on me in a lazy way. I forget that my body needs sunshine. I forget there are people in Africa fighting to survive. I forget because I'm trying to survive, too. I forget that I want to survive, sometimes. I forget to try, sometimes, too. I forget myself, when it might be more effective to forgive myself.

But what is there to forgive? What grudge am I holding against myself. I wish this was morning so I could just write all this angst out of me. Then I'd go home and feel accomplished and tired and I'd pray and grab some Subway and eat the whole sub and feel even more good about myself and then jump into bed. Middle of the day, jump into bed. Shut the blinds, into the bed. Covers over my head, into the bed. Transport to another plane of existence, one where time doesn't mean anything. Where the darkness consumes me and I am okay with that. Where I can just be the nothing I feel inside me. A chronic emptiness that often resurges at the worst time. A lingering sense of incompletion. That I make myself forget about. But things like that won't let you. They won't let you. Let you go.

Let me go, I wish they would have let me go. I wish they didn't drag me into King County Correctional. Wish I didn't have to do two years of probation, tricking my PO. All the drugs I done sold. Even more went up my nose. All the friends I left froze. In the streets, call it overdose. All the times I thought I was better off dead. Thought I was headed for it, right? Thought wrong. Thought to the left. Listening to the same old song. Same old Nacho Picasso. I said where's my gun? My gun said you don't own one.

I know that I have things in me that I wish I could change, but this is not me being sad. This is me indulging the things which make me who I am. I know people who say they would be happy to call me a friend. I believe that about myself, sometimes, but not always. You know what I mean?

I have a family who cares about me, and I them, on most days. I mean, love is unconditional, right? You can't walk away from family. Might still be mad at me. But we still blood, thicker than, had to be. Uhhh. Water.

I'm from Seattle where people drown in the rain, heads tilted back, eyes cloudy with the grey of the sky. In Seattle, we cry so many tears that they evaporate on our face and turn into clouds and produce the rain that is responsible for everyone being so depressed and crying on the back of the bus all the time.

In Seattle I would sit in the back of the bus, stumbled onto it. In Seattle I would watch my reflection in the windows, and the mist on the outside of the bus, leaving drops of condensation on that pane like the pain in me, like the tears on my face. Like the tears of a clown.

In Seattle I used to eat Pagliacci, like the theater clown. But life is no game, ain't no time for play-play. You hit that Dougie? I hit that Shanaynay.

BREAK.

THE FUGEES – TURN YOUR LIGHTS DOWN LOW

Judson — 3 years ago
never forget my mom holding me late at night and singing this song to me... never take anyone for granted.. i would give anything to feel her arms around me again and start bouncing me side to side to that "everything's gonna be alright, oh ahh oh ah oh ah..."

188 Likes. See 8 Replies.

BREAK.

I grew up with the internet. I mean, as the internet grew, so did I. First computer, 1999. White CRT. Big tower. NetZero dialup; it was free. 6th grade. Far cry from what these kids have now.

Too much power, too little hands.

Like a kid on the corner with the burner strapped. Ready to take a life, or have it took.

POW. Gun smoke.

But that's what America does to you. Makes you want to die. And pretend to want to take a life. Just so you might get caught in a position where you get your life took. And the block can memorialize you. Ribbons and teddy bears surrounding the light post you got shot at. The light post you used to sell that work at. Used to get beat at. And sometimes beat others.

And often beat feet from the siren's police.

Look, Juelz Santana said, "Wayne, I see your pain and I feel your stress. How they thinking people posed to get through Katrina offa FEMA checks?"

That's a valid question, because those checks never came. And if they did, too little, too late.

Like me getting up at noon to start my day.

Or me judging myself after the fact.

Or me judging the fact that I'm judging myself.

It's an endless loop. I'm in therapy, you know?

It's helping, I think.

I think.

I feel like I'm about to

BREAK.

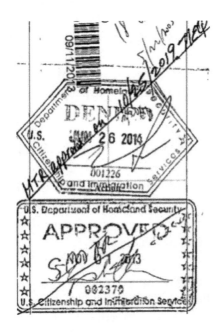

Some of the students I've taught were born and raised in America. Others, born elsewhere. It's easy to understand why grammar and punctuation mistakes can come from a person whose third language is English. But for someone who's native tongue it is, I always ask myself why? Why do you feel so entitled and better than the next man over, the one who came from nothing and taught themselves everything? Why do you feel better than someone who has a better grasp of "your" language than you do? Ignorance comes in many tongues. Some of them

BREAK.

I remember living somewhere between Ballard and I want to say Magnolia. It was a young-ish hipster neighborhood. It was about a year after I'd gotten over my post-dropout depression. I was working full time as a door to door salesman. I was hard drinking. I was living even harder. My roommate was Israeli. Former IDF guy. He was an alcoholic, too. Eventually he kicked me out because of my alcoholism, allegedly. I think there was more to it than that. It was weird that I found myself surrounded by Israelis. Because they knew I was supposed to be Muslim. I am Muslim. I was Muslim, just lost. I always wanted to be accepted. My whole life. I don't know how I ended up in their circle. Seattle is a weird place. White people are so bad for the health of a person of color in this country. Anyway.

I remember listening to a lot of The Strokes back then. Sonic Youth, too. I wasn't really into them, I mean, I hadn't grown up listening to them. But I liked them at the time. And I was around people who more or less appreciated them. I was with an indie crowd. I used to feel ashamed about that. I read Hanif Abdurraqib and he talks proudly about that. So I guess now I feel less ashamed about being a Black former pop punk indie emo fan. Generally speaking, I'm learning that shame has no useful place in my life. Old habits die hard.

It's been a long time since I wrote just to enjoy writing. For the fun of it. Here I am, coffee in hand, pounding away these sentences. The weight of the words feels like weight being lifted from me. I'm listening to SOMA right now, by The Strokes. I remember being in SOFA, San Francisco. I remember showing up to open mics at bars, hoping to spit. They never appreciated my work. I used to think I was too avant garde for them. I don't know how true that is. Maybe it's just because I'm Black and they expect me to be illiterate, expect every move I make to be a mistake, not deliberate.

My work has always been pretty decent (might even say good on a self-confident day). I'm lying. My work has always had fire. It's gotten more refined over the years, but the fire has always been there. Because the fire comes from within. And that's not something you can teach. The fire is pain, and pain you can't teach. Like a man on a football field – so much of what he does can't be taught. It's remembered in the genetics. The desire to free captivity by any means. Like Kodak said, "it's that fire." To escape is to release oneself from the fire.

Look man, forget all that. I got a girl who cares about me in my life. Never thought the day would come. Someone who won't leave me no matter how hard I try to make her leave. It's a trip.

I don't know what this work is, or what it'll turn into. I just know that it's here, it's something which needed to come from me. And I haven't walked away from it. The format has changed, and I don't want to peg it down as anything per se. *I just want to make it, bro.* I just want to get published. I know that's not going to solve any problems for me. I know it won't make things better. I know that it won't provide me lasting happiness or anything like that. But it'll be a major accomplishment that I've been working towards in so many ways for so many years. It's something which I can hold onto forever. And, knowing myself, it's something which I'll casually disregard shortly after it happens. I have a short-term memory. I make myself forget. A habit of dis-remembering. It's a survival tactic where I come from.

Where I come from, the people I know, they don't speak about their problems.

We hold them in until they fester & swell.

Until they consume us like fire. We let our problems burn like an Usher song.

You can see our faces, like a snapchat filter, the gap between fact and fiction.

The people I cling to cling to the word SOMEDAY as a means to a way.

The people I love don't very often know that I love them. I rarely tell them. Even more rarely show them. But they know, them. They know.

The people who love me have spent a lifetime showing me that they love me, but not always – or maybe never – being able to actually say it. Very rarely.

It's not a part of our culture. It's not who we are. We don't speak our demons. We bury them.

They eat away at us, dissolve us, like bones in a bottle of coca cola.

Someday, they say.

Someday I'll get my act together. Stop being abusive to my body. Stop treating those I care about like they owe me a debt. Even if they do, Someday, I'll get to a place where I don't ask them to repay that debt.

Someday I'll be okay.
We'll all be okay.

> Oh, someday....
> No, I ain't wasting
> No more tiiiiiiiiiiiime

—THE STROKES, SOMEDAY.

——Dear Said Farah:

You recently visited our information counter at your local field office and requested information about reopening your N-600 application. After reviewing the file and application, it has been determined that you will need to file an I-290B (Motion to Reopen) before we can take any further action on the application. The Form I-290B and instructions can be found at our website: www.uscis.gov/forms. We look forward to reopening your application.

Sincerely,

So, I'm going to stop doing the back and forth thing for a while (in all honesty, I haven't been sticking to the rules of this game I made for a while now, anyway). That's fine, I'm okay with it. I hope you can be, too.

What's on my mind? Feelings of inadequacy and failure. I'm extremely discouraged by submitting my pieces for publishing, spending money I don't have on the fees, only to be met with heartless rejections. It doesn't make sense – is this a test? I grow to love and hate writing in so many ways. Writing has never been a problem, when I wrote on my own terms. Things became difficult when I started trying to show my writing to the world.

So I'm out here just shooting my shot on Submittable and all I get back is a whole lotta nada. What does that mean, that I'm a terrible writer? Or that I should just stop submitting? How do I get around this hurdle?

I think the real question is: why am I submitting at all? What am I hoping to get out of it? Because what I'm getting back right now is negative. It's making me not want to write, to disbelieve in my writing – and I"ll be real with ya, I didn't need much help for that in the first place.

I'm living in a box now. I'm comparing myself to the best of the best – people who have been writing and sending for decades. People with PhDs and stringent understandings of what "good" writing is expected to look like. People who know the rules and are able to play by them. But none of those people have my experience. How many survivors of civil war, childhood trauma, colonialism, American poverty, racism and Islamophobia are writing the way I am? I bet you it's not very many, because most of them are trying to heal from the pain of their past. It just so happens that this is my way of healing, or at least, coming to terms with.

Why submit writing? Because it's what you're supposed to do, as a writer. You can't call yourself a writer if you are not ready for people to read that writing. I mean, that's why I have the blog. But the blog is like my little secret. Elusive. A treasure trove. Or a glimpse of one, I should say. I got a lot more writing on my laptop. And I don't necessarily feel good about having this secret stash. I don't think it's trash – or maybe I do. Maybe I'm tired of getting my feelings hurt so I decided to keep all this writing in hiding -even from myself. It's important to note that my relationship with writing is like my memory – I make myself forget things to survive. Always forever never remembering. And then I decided to write memoir, I guess as a natural antidote to my self-erasure.

No matter how much I learn about this craft, or how long I do it, or how seriously I commit to it, the feelings of never being good enough have yet to go away. Established writers tell me that feeling never goes away. I guess that's what makes us writers. The question is how do we survive those feelings and keep living?

My therapist tells me I'm self-invalidating. I don't like my therapist because they're always supposed to be right and always make me feel wrong. Something about therapy is very wrong.

I used to love sharing my writing with friends. Now I feel alone. I forgot why I wrote in the first place. I'm typing into a hollow box and the negative thoughts are hard to overcome. They consume. Like a fire, they burn.

You get me?

PRIORITY DATE
September 11, 2013

Please come to:
US CITIZENSHIP & IMMIGRATION SERVICES
12500 TUKWILA INTERNATIONAL BLVD
SEATTLE, WA 98168
SECOND FLOOR, ROOM1, GATE1

On (Date):   Tuesday, March 11 2014
At (Time):   8:30 AM

My Voice.

How can I be of assistance, sir?

Something just came un-shook in my brain piece. No peace.

You said you loved this girl, why are you second-guessing it?

I'm not. It just, really, really, hurts.

No one said this would be easy.

I want her to be in my life. Badly. But I am so broke. I can't afford a wedding or furniture.

Allah has provided you with everything you've ever asked Him. Why would He stop now?

This much is true, but I never thought any of those things would happen.

Oh ye of little faith.

My faith certainly isn't where it used to be. It's on the upswing now, but.

There is no but. You should try and be grateful. It would serve you better.

I agree. I want to be with this woman, but I fear that I won't be able to provide her with what she needs.

Every woman wants a fancy wedding. Of some kind. And you know it would mean a lot to her.

I just wish I could convince her to see things my way.

Why don't you try seeing things her way? Is your way the only way?

No, but I would prefer it. In my head it's like, "if you don't see things my way, you don't love me."

That's not rational.

No, like a freight train stacked with semi-truck trailers. It don't make no sense.

Your dad drives a truck, doesn't he?

In the winter, through snow, through danger, risking his life for some dream.

What dream is that?

To retire in Africa and never have to worry about money again. And just live in the sun.

And have his children send him money like the good Muslims he raised you to be?

Yeah, but we also grew up with a scarcity mentality.

Is that his fault?

Not really. Living in refugee camps does that to everyone; we're all victims. My shoulder hurts.

Why?

This chair is not quite as tall as I like for it to be in relation to the height of the desk. And if I lean forward, that's only gonna put extra strain on my back.

You are so peculiar.

Imagine how hard its been for me to find someone who accepts all of my idiosyncrasies.

You are really moving, now, Slim, you're writing like a wave.

It's the soundtrack to my life, the clack of the keys.

Tell me what your biggest dream is?

I guess I haven't thought of that in a long time. I guess I'm living a version of it.

So now it's time to re-calibrate. What's your new dream?

Voice, make it to the top!

Cream gotta rise baby.

You already know. I ran so hard and fast towards these goals that I found myself standing on top of them.

So you already made it. Now where do you want to go?

Start a family, get married, not in that order.

Why does your shoulder hurt so much?

I feel tense. It might be a sign that I'm avoiding something.

Why don't you go get a massage?

Let me look into that, brb.

20 minutes later Let me guess…

Yeah, I didn't find anything out. But. I'm back now, so. There's that.
I'm proud of you, bro. I hope you know that.

Thank you, Voice. That means a lot coming from you.

I feel like you've made a lot of progress in a few short weeks of DBT.

I'm in recovery, baby. I'm tryna be the man of my dreams. Man of my wife-to-be's dreams.

I think you are who you've always been. But you're just getting better at refining him.

I agree. I'm not sure what this means for me and my future, but I know that this beat is riding hard and the snow outside is drifting slow and my coffee is sitting middle-low and I be on it.

What you be on?

On my grind. Look, I gotta go.

Look, don't stress about the wedding. It'll work out for the best, Insha Allah.

I know bro. I just get so discouraged and upset and impatient, and she gets impatient too, cuz we just wanna be together.

I know. But you've waited this long. She's not going anywhere, please stop trying to chase her away.

She be doing the same thing, too, tho.

Yeah, but can you blame her? Everyone gets insecure about marriage, especially. How many guys have come up to her professing love and talking marriage and just walked right out of her life?

Yeah, they get it worse than we do. I'm a guy, I might hurt, but I'll make it out. She was about to throw up after our last argument. She felt it in her body.

That could be the future mother of your children, bro. Be easy to her.

I know, I'm trying, but we're both so frustrated by our situation.

It's Qadr of Allah. Show patience. Sabr. You'll be rewarded for it.

I know, bro, but it's hard to remember that when the emotions are flying high.

We are human. We were created impatient and anxious. This is your nature. You have to try and rise above that.

I am trying, bro.

What did brother therapist man say the other week – I know you're trying hard, but that's not enough anymore. You have to keep lifting.

Permission to break form, Sir?

Granted.

Ok. I haven't eaten lunch and it's 3:20 PM and I'm not hungry (actually I am), but I don't want to stop writing. I don't want to stop drinking coffee. I don't want this scene to end. It's perfect. I feel like I won't be able to get back to this place again. It takes so much work just to get myself here, and I know all I want to do is write, but I'm self-invalidating so often, that the only thought that comes into my head (immediately following the urge to write) is: what's the point? You won't do anything with it, anyway. But I will. I got that funky cold medina.

I don't know what that means, but I got the fire in me. And it needs to come out. I left my headlights on, every night before I went to sleep, for about a year and my battery never died. My heart is still pumping. My eyes are still bleary. My girl still loves me. My family still supports me, and I'm not talking about money. My money is no longer long but I have more than I've ever dreamed. And I might not have enough to get married at this present moment. But at least I don't have withdrawals. And I got these beautiful 10-dollar co-pays no matter how much the service costs. I'm in two different therapies, bro. Look, man what I'm trying to say is I somehow love my life, at this very present moment, and I know a lot of that has to do with the hyping myself up that happens when I write – and I'm just now realizing that it's very similar to bodybuilders yelling and screaming before they get under all that weight and just lift. I have to hype myself up to lift this weight. To write these words, you can't just show up casually. You gotta slap yourself across the street. Or slap your brother across the face. Or chase your own tail. I ain't no dog though. Woof.

I'm happiest when I'm sitting at the table to write and the coffee is going strong. I don't want the feeling to end. Sometimes you have to sacrifice temporary personal comfort for the greater good of your wellbeing. I'm loving the snow flying sideways on the wind outside this window.

* * *

USCIS
Form I-290B
OMB No. 1615-0095
Expires 05/31/2020

Sometimes I just lay in bed and stare at nothing, feeling like nothing, feeling the nothing weight of my body, feeling like my mind is there but not. Feeling like I'm here but somewhere else, too.

Congratulations! Your application for Form N-600, Certificate of Citizenship, has been approved. However, all persons age 14 or older are required to take an Oath of Allegiance to the United States prior to the issuance of a Certificate of Citizenship. You have been scheduled for an ADMINISTRATION OF OATH at the time and place listed below. It is important that you be early or on time for this appointment. The appointment will begin at the time indicated below.

Address: U.S Citizenship and Immigration Services
250 Marquette Ave, Suite 710
Minneapolis, MN 55401

Date: Tuesday, December 17, 2019

Time: 1:30 pm

You must surrender your alien registration card (and any United States travel documents) at this appointment. Bring this notice, your alien registration card (and travel documents), and if your alien registration card was issued more than ten years ago, recent legal photo identification (i.e. a driver's license or passport) to the appointment. Please be advised, proper identification is also required to enter the building.

✳ ✳ ✳

I jump outside and stretch my body because sometimes sentences get stuck between my shoulder blades and need to be shook loose. Like a loose shake joint, wrapped between a piece of thin paper. What does that even mean to me anymore – I mean, what am I supposed to do with all that experience? I don't smoke anymore, so what does the knowledge of how to roll the perfect blunt – or joint – translate to my now-sober life? It really doesn't, but I wonder. What can I do with all that old skill? I could go for a run, right now. I really need a run.

Update: I unwrapped myself in a run, and it was magnificent.

BREAK.

When I first started this project, I wasn't sure what I wanted it to be. In many ways, I still haven't answered that question. I was in a different emotional space when I began. I was in fight or flight mode, struggling to breathe during my first semester in the MFA. One of the only things keeping me going was not knowing what this project could be. I didn't want to cap it. No self-limitations. It was exciting and fresh and served a purpose for me that I couldn't have gotten in any other way. When my social support network failed to understand what I was going through, this project gave me the legs to walk into a space of breathing. A breath space. A diaphragm unfolding. A stomach un-holding.

I've also been plagued by a need to write a memoir of trauma. But the memoir is not wanting to be written. And so the need to write it grows stronger. One of my professors told me that it might be useful to think about the question at the heart of the memoir, and that the question will open the door for the structure of the memory to fall into place. So what's the question? Easy. Who/ What/How Am I?

I guess I've been so focused on the very act of writing THE MEMOIR that I haven't looked at the underlying questions. Why do I need to write this story? Why did I go down the paths that I did? Why did I find my way back to writing, time and again? What role does writing serve in my wholeness, and how did it let me get there? And faith. What about faith?

I often wonder where I would be in this world if not for my faith.

I see what's happening to Muslim kids today and I think back to the worst of my days. In many ways, it would appear that they're headed for the same paths. Only God knows what end they'll meet. But from where I'm sitting, I have a combination of remorse for my own past, fear for their future (and, by extension, the future of my own children), and a bunch of other things.

As one who submits to God, I feel responsible for the upliftment of my community. I want us to do good, to win. I want all of us to enter heaven, to abstain from sin. But this time in the world is making it very easy to do wrong, very hard to do right. Of course, life wasn't meant to be easy, but still.

Even after everything I've experienced in my life, I still wonder where I'd be if not for my faith.

Living with a chronic mental health condition is no small task. But what choice do I have but to live that life? And where would I be, if not for my faith and my community? Who would I be? No one, no thing, that's who, that's what.

And I'm out.

Peace.

Oath of Allegiance

Department of Homeland Security
U.S. Citizenship and Immigration Services

**USCIS
Form G-1222**

USCIS A-Number

A-

I hereby declare, on oath,[1] that I absolutely and entirely renounce and abjure all allegiance and fidelity to any foreign prince, potentate, state, or sovereignty, of whom or which I have heretofore been a subject or citizen; that I will support and defend the Constitution and laws of the United States of America against all enemies, foreign and domestic; that I will bear true faith and allegiance to the same; ~~that I will bear arms on behalf of the United States when required by the law; that I will perform noncombatant service in the Armed Forces of the United States when required by the law;~~[2] that I will perform work of national importance under civilian direction when required by the law; and that I take this obligation freely, without any mental reservation or purpose of evasion; so help me God.

GRATITUDE

(The Big Thank You List)

There are so many people who this project would not be possible without. Even if they didn't directly help in this particular piece of writing, they have been instrumental in everything that led me to this point. A writer is nothing without his community, and I am no exception.

First, I give thanks to Allah SWT & I ask that He send peace and blessings upon our Beloved Prophet Muhammad (Peace Be Upon Him). I ask that He assist our Ummah through every trial we are facing and I ask that He forgive us for our shortcomings and bless us all with heaven everlasting, Amiin. Any benefit that comes from this book is from Him and Him Alone. Any shortcoming is from my own deficiency and from the whisperings of the Shaytaan. I love you, Allah. Thank you, for everything. Thank you for saving me from so many vices and traps, so many pitfalls and tar pits. Thank you for blessing me with a second, third, fourth chance at life. Thank you for never giving up on me, and always guiding me, even when I was foolish enough to think I didn't need it. You have always been there for me, and a lifetime of worship would not be even remotely close enough to showing you my gratitude. May you forgive me, and may you bless us all with heaven everlasting. Allahuma Amiin.

I also want to thank my family: Hooyo Safia Hassan Jama, Aabe Mahad Farah Shaiye, Sisters Lebin, Ladan and Leyla. Brothers Abdi and Liban. Rest in Peace to my baby sister Najma who never made it out of Somalia with us. I pray we get to meet in heaven. Thank you, family, for never giving up on me, for always being there for me, even when I pushed you away. We have been through a lot together – criss-crossed the world for what feels like several lifetimes, all the while clinging to each other like the crew aboard *Voyager*. Our family was my *Voyager*, and I pray heaven is the Earth that we are journeying towards. Please forgive me for my shortcomings, and for the nights I kept you awake, worried for my safety while I was out dealing with my demons. Hey, being a child of civil war isn't an easy thing to contend with. You gotta survive however you can in this country. But you already know that.

I want to thank my brother, mentor, co-conspirator and all around inspirational human being Doug Kearney. I wouldn't be half the man I am (and becoming) had Allah not seen fit to cross our paths. You saved me from leaving my MFA program when the going got tough (day 1, I was sweating). You pushed me to believe in myself. You would not accept any self-deprecating or self-doubting talk from me. Well, you let me say my piece, then you gently reminded me of all the things I had to be grateful for, and all that I had to offer my people, my community, the world at large. Look, I'm about to start crying as I type this, lmao. But I love you, man. You're the type of person I've always aspired to be more like – free in their art & always putting people first. Without people like you, this world would be a much darker place. And I give you my gratitude.

To my dear friend Khadijo Abdi, thank you a million times over. You have been there for me in more ways than I can count. You believed in me from the day we met. You helped me become a medical interpreter, something that I thought was my dream. We're allowed to have multiple dreams, you know? That's something we've been learning together. And we've grown together, and hoped together, and I can't picture my life without you. I truly cannot. I pray Allah SWT blesses you with everything good in this life and the next, and I pray all your dreams (writing & otherwise) come true very, very soon. I can't wait for the world to experience how amazing of a writer and (more importantly to me) person you are. I wouldn't be here without you, know that I love you. And I pray we get to meet in heaven when all this is said and done. PS -- Don't let Guled slap you around anymore. You deserve better. From your cat. Lol.

To my boy Donald Quist, what can I say? Our friendship started out with a fan-boy email I sent you after reading your essay *The Souls of Latarian Milton* on Lithub. I was a miserable medical interpreter, reading essays to pass the time. Your words cut into me like a scalpel. I stopped everything I was doing and felt so transported to your world that I felt we'd been friends for a lifetime. Everything I know to be true of you screams YOUR FAVORITE WRITER'S

FAVORITE WRITER. You are truly dedicated to this craft, in ways I can only hope to one day reach. You are someone I hold in such high regard, who has been so kind to me, and supportive, in so many ways. I'll never forget our Waffle House adventure on my road trip, eating those chicken biscuit sandwiches in 10 degree weather on the parking lot of the La Quinta in Columbia, Missouri. You a real one, bro, and I'm so grateful to have you in my life.

To Kathryn Nuernberger, thank you for all your support in helping me get a better grasp of what it means to be a writer in a professional sense – applying for grants and residencies and learning the rhetorical language of these things is such critical knowledge. Thank you, as well, for always believing in my work and pushing me forward with encouragement. Thank you, as well, for helping me develop a less traumatic way of teaching. Even if I never go on to teach, it's good to know that I wasn't the problem, but the system.

To Geoff Herbach, thank you for your support over the years. Ever since we met in Mankato, you've been a trusted friend and mentor. As mentioned in my book, I've had a lot of issues with self-doubt and you were one of the people who's helped me push past that – or, just learn to accept it as part of being a writer. And that there's nothing wrong with that.

To Barracuda Guarisco & Kelsey Harris, thank you for being the first to believe in this book. Really Serious Literature will forever be in my heart. I like to think I'm a rapper sometimes. I know I'm not, but I like to think it. Anyway, all my favorite rappers shun the major record labels and go indie. They do it for the sake of the craft, to better themselves and reach the people. They don't want a million hands meddling in their rap-stew, so they make it rap-do what it rap-do. Y'all my indie label, and I'll forever rock with you in some capacity or other. If I wasn't Muslim, and if getting tattoos wasn't against my religion, I'd get RSL tatted. Squad.

To my boys Abdimalik Ahmed & Abdimalik Mohamed & Suleiman Adan – dawg, what can I say? You've shown me the true meaning of brotherhood in Islam. Never wavering, you've always shown love to me & never judged me like our culture teaches us to do. Y'all have the biggest hearts of anyone I've met and I thank Allah for putting us in each other's lives. I only pray I've been a fraction of the friend you've shown yourselves to be.

And to all the other brothers in this weird MPLS Somali/East African/Black Muslim community – thank you. I'm sorry if things have gotten weird between us, I have a lot of relationship issues. Call it a side effect of civil war. I know that's not an excuse, but damn, I'm trying lol. I pray Allah forgives me if I've burnt a bridge with you, and I pray you do, too. I'm far from perfect, but I'm also just trying to survive. Solitude is all I know.

To my sisters Diana Diaz & Rowena Chodkowski – VONA kicked my ass and made me almost-hate writing, but getting you two out of that experience more than makes up for it. Y'all have been there, and I know I keep saying this about everyone, but I mean you have *been there* for me. Thank you for all your care, for always seeing me, and for never trying to make me anything I wasn't ready for or interested in being.

To Dr. Saido Abdi, Habo, thank you thank you thank you. You always say I'm about to make you cry with my crazy life stories, but you are such an important part of my life. You specialize in trauma, and you have honored my trauma in ways that no one else has before I met you. You have taught me to be kinder to myself, and you have taught me not to think everyone was one mistake away from abandoning me. You are a blessing, a light, in my life, and I pray Allah SWT rewards you for all the good you have done. Thank you also to our RA team on the Somali Mental Health project – Anisa, Sarita, Safiya, Sofiya, Subeyda, and Zaynab. Y'all are the best.

Thanks also to every girl that broke my heart or generally antagonized me in weird ways during the writing of this. You know who you are, lol. It's all love. Wish you the best and all that. And I'm sorry to every girl whose time I wasted, and vice versa.

And thank you, dear reader, for getting on this journey with me. Thank you to anyone I forgot to thank – if you know me, you know how terrible my memory is. Just another side effect of childhood trauma, man, forgive me. If you mean something to me, or have meant something to me (even if I arbitrarily burnt out bridge), please know that you have my gratitude. And if I die before we get to reconcile, or whatever, please forgive me. I pray for you how I hope you pray for me.

And I pray that Allah SWT forgives us all. Be kind to yourselves, and remember that Allah is with you, if no one else.

Asalaamu Alaikum Wa Rahmatullahi Wa Barakaatahu.

SAID SHAIYE is a writer of Somali descent who grew up in Seattle and now calls Minneapolis home. He is a survivor of childhood trauma and adulthood addiction. He has had work published in *Entropy, Diagram, 580 Split, Night Heron Barks, Muslim American Writers at Home,* and elsewhere. *Are You Borg Now?* is his debut book. He can be reached at www.saidshaiye.com.

CPSIA information can be obtained
at www.ICGtesting.com
Printed in the USA
BVHW011032110921
616283BV00006B/30

9 780578 915463